D1487964

Stanley Tam's Incredible Adventures with God

Dr. R. Stanley Tam
as told to Ken Anderson

CHRISTIAN PUBLICATIONS, INC.
CAMP HILL, PENNSYLVANIA

CHRISTIAN PUBLICATIONS, INC.
3825 Hartzdale Drive, Camp Hill, PA 17011
www.christianpublications.com

Stanley Tam's Incredible Adventures with God
ISBN: 0-88965-211-2
© 2002 by R. Stanley Tam
All rights reserved
Printed in the United States of America

02 03 04 05 06   5 4 3 2 1

Unless otherwise indicated,
Scripture taken from the HOLY BIBLE:
NEW INTERNATIONAL VERSION ®.
Copyright © 1973, 1978, 1984 by the
International Bible Society. Used by
permission of Zondervan Bible Publishers.

Scripture references labeled "KJV"
are taken from the Holy Bible:
King James Version

Scripture references labeled "NKJV" are taken from
The Holy Bible, New King James Version,
Copyright © 1982 by Thomas Nelson, Inc.
The New King James Bible, New Testament
Copyright © 1979 by Thomas Nelson, Inc.
The New King James Bible, New Testament and Psalms
Copyright © 1980 by Thomas Nelson, Inc.

Scripture labeled "TLB" is taken from
The Living Bible: Paraphrased, © 1971
by Tyndale House Publishers. All rights reserved.

Dedication

This book is dedicated to my son-in-law,
Jack Williams, who married my oldest daughter,
Rachel. God took him home to heaven in the
prime of his life. He was a devoted Christian,
a student of Greek, a partner in a civil
engineering firm. We all miss him, but rejoice
over his victory to be with his Savior.

Also to our four daughters and three sons-in-law,
Rachel, Becky, Wes, Prudy, Darrell, Candy, Paul,
our grandchildren, Heather, Bryan and Heather Ann,
Stuart, Sarah, Stanley, Jennifer and Chris, Kristin,
Michele, Paul J. and Peter,
our two great grandchildren, Aubry and Jack,
and of course Juanita, my dear companion
of sixty-three years.
Our life verse for our family is a wonderful promise,
please make it yours.

Seek ye first the kingdom of God, and his righteousness;
and all these things shall be added unto you.
(Matthew 6:33, KJV)

CONTENTS

Preface..ix

CHAPTER ONE
How Dr. D. James Kennedy Told My Story.......................................1

CHAPTER TWO
The Wandering Tams Settle Down...8

CHAPTER THREE
I Could Have Become a Farmer...12

CHAPTER FOUR
My First Cigarette—and Last 18

CHAPTER FIVE
Depression Scars...23

CHAPTER SIX
Model T Mania 26

CHAPTER SEVEN
The Greatest of All Miracles..30

CHAPTER EIGHT
Afterglow 40

CHAPTER NINE
Entering a New World 46

CHAPTER TEN
Looking for a Job..53

CHAPTER ELEVEN
Lessons to Learn 59

CHAPTER TWELVE
At the Crossroads 66

CHAPTER THIRTEEN
Needs Supplied, Wants Granted 72

CHAPTER FOURTEEN
The Girl from Rockford 76

CHAPTER FIFTEEN
Old-Fashioned Romance 82

CHAPTER SIXTEEN
Honeymoon Business Trip 87

CHAPTER SEVENTEEN
Beginning a Family 92

CHAPTER EIGHTEEN
Business Unusual 100

CHAPTER NINETEEN
Our World "Market" 118

CHAPTER TWENTY
The OMS International Story 126

CHAPTER TWENTY-ONE
Life's Greatest Goal—Winning Souls 129

CHAPTER TWENTY-TWO
Cancer Crisis 150

CHAPTER TWENTY-THREE

Sunsets and Horizons 156

EPILOGUE

Laying Up Treasures in Heaven...162

How to Receive the Gift of Eternal Life
and Become a Vital New Person...176

Preface

Next to Christ, the most influential man in my life has been Ken Anderson, a renowned author, producer of award-winning Christian films and a promoter of spiritual media to foreign missions. I first met him when we both served on the board of Youth for Christ International, located in Wheaton, Illinois. Back in the '60s, one night across the table at dinner, Ken said, "Stanley, I would like to write a book about you." The result was *God Owns My Business*, which now has over 400,000 copies in print in eight languages.

Following the writing of the book, Ken produced two motion pictures, the first being "God Owns My Business," and the second, "The Answer." Then came the four-film series "Adventures in Soul Winning," and two more books, *Every Christian a Soul Winner* and *God's Woodshed*.

With his winsome smile, he would always say, "I will gladly write it (or produce it) at no cost, just for the honor of doing it." He would accept a token far below what his talent and labor was worth. He has that ability to make a message from every instance. His efforts have catapulted me onto the front lines of the war between the Lord and the devil over the souls of men, and together we have seen thousands of souls come to Christ as Savior.

Dr. R. Stanley Tam

ONE

How Dr. D. James
Kennedy Told My Story

One of my cherished friends, especially in the ministry of soul-winning, is Dr. D. James Kennedy, pastor of the beautiful Coral Ridge Presbyterian Church in Fort Lauderdale, Florida. As the founder and director of Evangelism Explosion, a worldwide fellowship of Christians involved in personal witness, he became interested in my book, *God Owns My Business*. As a consequence, he preached a sermon titled "What Is a Stanley Tam?" in the cathedral-like sanctuary of his television-outreach church.

It seemed ideal for me to have Dr. Kennedy introduce this autobiography, not only due to his renown and the honor of being recognized by a man of such stature but, more so, because of the warmth and expertise with which he crafted the gist of my story into a pulpit presentation.

The following are the abridged words of Dr. Kennedy's sermon from that televised Sunday morning message at Coral Ridge.

What in the world is a Stanley Tam? Is it a Stanley Steamer? That's something people have been asking me since I announced my sermon topic for this week.

It's not a thing at all. It's a person.

Stanley Tam is just an average man—average in mentality, average in physical endowments—and yet a man who has discovered one of the secrets of God that has led to enormous blessing in his life.

He didn't set out years ago to be some kind of nonconformist or spiritual hippy. He is just an average, rational, reasonable human being. Though he is but an average type of person, with the endowments of an average individual, he cannot understand how many Christians can read the Bible, which abounds in many promises to them—promises to make their lives far beyond the average—and yet settle for a spiritual vitality so mediocre as to seem virtually nonexistent. As a result of mediocre spiritual vitality being the norm, the Christian who becomes demonstrably involved with God is looked upon as the rare exception, far above the established rule. But it is Stanley's conviction that this full and rewarding life is everyone's birthright. We deny God's best for us by our own default.

What is the discovery Stanley Tam made?

Well, you might say it's the discovery of a life that is full, life at its best, life as God meant it to be. That discovery came when he learned a life-changing truth.

"I believe tenaciously," he says, "in the possibility of a man linking his life to God."

He makes it very plain in his book *God Owns My Business* that the way he has linked his life to God has been God's unique leading with him personally. He never encourages others to emulate him but, instead, he urges them to seek God's guidance in their own lives. His method is his own—the principle is for everyone.

And that principle can change your life.

"I believe tenaciously in the possibility of a man linking his life to God."

What does that mean to the man who said it, and how did it happen?

R. Stanley Tam was born near San Francisco in 1915. By the time he became a teenager the depression was setting in. He was a young man with a strong drive to be a success as a salesman, to make money and to make good. Those were his goals in life, and yet he was very diffident, shy and timid— weaknesses with which he struggled for years. He would try anything to make some money in those difficult days, and would sell just about anything he could get his hands on. He learned many lessons during that time.

For example, he bought an old Model T Ford for a few dollars, fixed it up and offered to sell it for $15, quite a handsome price in those days. The first man that answered his ad agreed to buy it for that price. Stanley was delighted. The man offered to pay five dollars down and the rest on installments. He then talked the young salesman into giving him the owner's certificate. As a naive young teenager, Stanley gave it to the deceitful man and never saw the remaining payment.

Stanley Tam learned early that people are sinful. He hadn't really learned that truth about himself, however, until a very charming woman told him about the love of Christ and the grace of God and the offer of eternal life to those who would place their trust in the crucified and risen Savior. Stanley, after much struggle, decided to do that very thing.

But Stanley's growth in the Christian life was slow at first. He had learned to trust Christ for his eternal life, and he slowly began to learn to trust Him for the things of this world and to help him overcome his shyness.

Still, he had a burning drive to be a success as a salesman. So he started a small business reclaiming silver washed off of film in photo-processing laboratories. He worked hard, eighteen hours a day, refining the reclaimed silver and traveling to serve present clients and enlist new ones.

But things got increasingly worse. One positive factor was that, on a business trip to Rockford, Illinois, he met Juanita, the young lady who became his wife. Marriage enriched his life, but although Juanita, a fine Christian, became an excellent partner, Stanley's business continued to worsen.

Finally, with all of his savings gone and just a few cents in his pocket, Stanley headed home from one of his trips in complete dejection. He pulled his car off the side of the road and cried out, "Oh, God! I'm finished! Broke. I've tried every way I know to make my business prosper. I've worked from sunup to sundown and I just can't make it. I need your help. Lord, I'm going to turn my business over to you."

A strange peace filled his heart. He knew God had heard his prayer. His business began to grow, and his promise to God kept coming back to him until finally, months later, he said to his wife, "You know, dear, there's something that's bothering me. I made a promise to God months ago that I was going to turn my business over to Him. He's been blessing me, and yet I've done nothing about that promise. I feel I must do something about it."

"What do you mean, dear?" his wife asked.

"Well," he replied, "I've prayed about it, and I've decided that I'm going to make God the senior partner of my firm."

"That's wonderful."

"I'm going to see a lawyer, have the papers drawn up and turn fifty-one percent of my business over to God."

"How will you do that?" Juanita asked.

"I will form a charitable foundation for the Lord's work," he answered.

3

So he went to a lawyer and presented his idea. The lawyer said, "That's absurd. I won't have anything to do with such a hair-brained idea."

Stanley was very shaken by this, so he went to another lawyer and said, "I'm just a normal human being. I love my wife. I have a business. I enjoy a good meal and a nice home, but I believe in God, and I believe He should be first in my life."

The lawyer said, "That's very commendable."

Encouraged, Stanley continued, "I want to turn over fifty-one percent of my business to God."

The lawyer looked at him, startled. When Stanley explained what he had in mind, the second lawyer voiced the same negative resistance as the first one had done. Stanley was puzzled. But he knew in his heart he had to do this. The lawyer told him he didn't have anything to turn over anyway and needed to think about building for retirement. "This is a terrible idea," the lawyer concluded.

Stanley went on and God continued to bless his life and his business so abundantly that before long he was able to return to his lawyer and persuade him of what he had in mind. The papers were drawn up and the Stanita Foundation—from Stanley and Juanita—was formed with the money to be used for the work of Jesus Christ.

Then a whole series of amazing things began to happen as Stanley experienced divine guidance. Events that could have been disastrous in the business were turned into tremendous new outlets and new sources of profit. He realized that God indeed does work all things "together for good to them that love God, to them who are the called according to his purpose" (Romans 8:28, KJV).

His business so prospered that people began to find out about it, and he was asked to speak at churches, clubs and the like.

God continued to bless him. He became convinced that God wanted him to do even more. So he went back to the lawyer and gave sixty percent of his company stock to God. Again the Lord blessed his business and it continued to expand. So he opened another plant. Other new sources of revenue appeared and the increases continued. He was spending a great deal of his time on the road speaking.

Stanley's primary interest was in missionary enterprises, so he and Juanita began taking speaking ministries overseas. One day in South America, having just finished giving his testimony to a congregation there, he had not yet stepped away from behind the pulpit at the end of the service when God suddenly seemed to speak to him and say, "Stanley, there is something more I want you to do. I want you to turn the business over to Me completely."

At that point, Stanley rebelled.

"Lord," he responded in distressed silence, "I've spent fifteen years of my life building this business. It means everything to me. I've poured my life's blood into it."

But the Lord seemed to say, "Stanley, there is something more in life than just making a living. You live in a comfortable home. You can only drive one car at a time; only wear one suit at a time. How much more do you want? Lift up your eyes, Stanley, and see the fields are white at the harvest. Just think what you could do for the kingdom of God if you are willing to turn your business over to me completely."

So, after much anguish and soul searching, Stanley returned to the lawyer and told him he wanted to turn the business entirely over to God—100 percent—and that he, the founder, would now become an employee for God in His business.

No sooner had he turned his entire business over to God, than Stanley decided that God was a far better businessman than he was, so he better make provisions for the work that God would do. The first thing Stanley did was enlarge his plant and storehouses by four times what they were before. He then waited to see God do His thing. The business began to boom and continued to grow. Stanley realized his responsibility was to collaborate with God in this world, that the earth was the Lord's and the fullness thereof.

The business continued to grow until it became a multimillion-dollar corporation with several different plants and outlets. Stanley realized that God was calling him to a life of obedience. God wanted him to be a witness so that people could see what a life completely turned over to God looked like. He knew he must be obedient in every detail.

One time, at the end of the year, as he was taking inventory he noticed a mistake on the silver cost, and that the company had made $4,000 more than they should have. That was a small amount and it came from 3,000 different customers, so at times it only amounted to around $1 a customer. Why bother trying to return the money? But the Lord kept saying to him, "Stanley, you've got $4,000 in your pocket that doesn't belong to you."

He argued, "But Lord, they are all different amounts. It would take weeks to figure out just how much should go to each person."

To which God said, "Stanley, that money is not yours."

Remembering his pledge of obedience, Stanley summoned his secretary and they spent six weeks doing detailed accounting, figuring out exactly how much of that money belonged to each customer. He got the checks ready and the Lord told him he needed to send out a statement explaining why he was returning the money. The people needed to know that God owned Stanley's business, and that Stanley was returning the money because he wanted nothing to in any way besmirch his testimony for God. So he sent out a letter of witness with each check.

To his amazement, he was flooded with letters of response from all over the country. People were astounded that they had received the money. From that gesture, all sorts of business potential resulted.

He reached the place where after taxes he was making a net profit of several million dollars per year, and he was able to support the work of Christ around the world in amazing ways. He discovered that God was quite able to fulfill His promise as He had said. Yes, there had been struggles, yes there had been testing, but in all of those trials Stanley had learned to trust God. God was able to supply all of Stanley's needs out of His riches in glory because Stanley had linked his life to God.

As Stanley has said, many people rob themselves of the blessing of God by their own default—by their own unbelief, by their unwillingness to trust God for this area of their lives and by their failure to prove Him and to find Him to be faithful. I can honestly say to you that as I have tried over the years to give more and more to the Lord, He has in turn opened many windows and poured more and more upon me. We have found, as Stanley found, that there is greater joy in life than making money or simply trying to be a success. There is the joy of sharing life itself in the name of Christ with other people.

Stanley discovered this in an incident he describes as how the Lord helped him overcome his shyness so he could share the good news of Christ with other people and to see first one, than another, then thousands of people come to know the love of Jesus Christ.

After three decades in business, Stanley was in his plant office when an elderly man came in on crutches. Resting the crutches across Stanley's desk, the elderly man said, "Mr. Tam, a customer of mine gave me your name and address. He told me he had discovered a secret from you, the secret of life eternal, and his life was so transformed and he found so much joy that I just felt I had to come and see you myself. As you can see, I'm in pretty bad shape, the doctors say I'm not going to live much longer and I'm not ready to die. Can you help me?"

Sensing something familiar about the man, Stanley asked, "Haven't we met before?"

"No," the man replied, "I know you speak all around, but I've never had the pleasure of hearing you."

Stanley shared with him the love that sent the Son of God to die upon the cross and the free gift of eternal life which God offers to those who put their trust in the crucified Savior. With tears in his eyes, the elderly man accepted the gift of eternal life. And he said, "Mr. Tam, how I wish I had known you earlier in my life. What pains I could have been spared."

In that moment, Stanley suspected the man's identity but said nothing.

The man grew increasingly ill in the months to come and was unable to work. Stanley helped him financially over those months.

"You are an answer from God to my life," the old fellow said one day. "How I wish I could have known you earlier." Stanley, about to speak, kept silent.

Then one day he received a telephone call informing him the man had died. Tears came to Stanley's eyes and he wept freely—not in sorrow for the man, whom he knew had gone to be with the Lord, but for joy that he had been privileged to lead the man to Christ. And he thought to himself, *One day in eternity, we will meet again.* Then the truth would be known. That man, converted in the sunset years of life, would make a discovery. He would learn that Stanley Tam, the man who led him to the Savior, was also the young man from whom he had purchased that old Model T for five dollars down payment, and then defrauded him out of the remainder due.

"I believe tenaciously," Stanley says, "in the possibility of a man linking his life to God and, in that linkage, discovering life as God means it to be."

The Wandering Tams Settle Down

Any way you figure it, Babe Ruth was a famous man. Even with the Mark McGwire and Sammy Sosa home run derby, his name endures.

Back in 1923, when I was eight years old, word spread across Lima that the great Bambino, the "Sultan of Swat," was coming to town. Together with a chattering throng of other boys, I dashed to the announced parade route. Moments later, a caravan appeared. In the back seat of a limousine sat the great home run hitter himself. Seeing us boys, he ordered his driver to stop, and he got out of the vehicle and came toward us. I forgot how to breathe or swallow for half a moment.

There he stood. The great and only George Herman "Babe" Ruth. He shook hands with most of the boys but I, hopelessly shy, didn't offer my hand. But I remember how excited I was, standing within reaching distance of the man I without question reckoned to be the most famous person on earth.

Well, I'm an octogenarian now, with my entire life pretty much behind me. The fact that you are reading my story attests to the fact of my being sufficiently well-known for a book to be written about my aspirations and achievements. Were it not for the book *God Owns My Business*, plus a couple of media presentations, I would be much less known than I am. Not that it matters, because I neither make any claim to fame nor have any desire whatsoever for celebrity status.

What I'm driving at is this: Ordinary though my life has been in many ways, a wonderful truth remains. You are reading this book and know about Stanley Tam not because I was a famous person like Babe Ruth. Nor is it because I gained a public image through politics or some other secular attainment. You are looking into my story—and I can tell you from my heart that you will be thrilled with what you find—because, through these eight decades of my life, a commoner from Lima somehow has had the sense to pay attention to the Bible and put its principles into practice through simple obedience to its teachings.

I can best attest to my desire to give God the glory by quoting a Bible verse impressed upon my mind and heart from the early days of my Christian experience: "God forbid that I should glory, save in the cross of our Lord Jesus Christ, by whom the world is crucified unto me, and I unto the world" (Galatians 6:14, KJV).

As I indicated earlier, I did have a terribly low self-image and was at times almost tormented by shyness during my early years. I was, in fact, so retiring some thought me backward. But say, friend, don't miss the point: God doesn't need people with an outgoing personality. He doesn't look for high IQs. What God is looking for are people, like you and me, who will give themselves—whatever we may be—completely into the Holy Spirit's control. Such attainment, for want of a better word, forces a man into humility and dependence.

But back to my boyhood days.

Through the years, Lima has remained the center point of Tam history. It was in Lima where my dad met a girl by the name of Hazel McBeth. Her parents were quite wealthy, so they looked askance at the young man with such limited resources who came courting. When asked what she saw in the young man, my mother replied, "He's wonderful, Father. He's all I ever dreamed or hoped for. I can't possibly imagine ever meeting someone who appeals to me more."

"I think you've got your head full of blabber talk," her father countered.

It was obvious there would be no parental blessing on their nuptials, although her father did not outright refuse to give his blessing. Taking no chances, however, my dad and Hazel eloped to Kentucky, then returned to Lima to make their home.

Just as I did in my early days, my father had a hard time settling into an occupation where he could provide the basic needs for a family. He seemed to be more of a follower than a leader.

Shyness may well have been a Tam's inherent weakness. Grandfather Tam seemed to have been somewhat henpecked, but he emerged a reasonably dynamic person, his strength stemming from the personality of his own father. For example, Grandfather Tam handled himself with expertise in public. He was an accomplished magician and gave performances during the days of vaudeville and early Chautauqua, with my dad serving as his assistant.

But, Grandfather Tam's eye was caught by the advent of the motion picture and he pretty much gave up magic to purchase a theater in the resort town of Russell's Point, about an hour's drive south and a tad east of Lima.

Business never thrived at the Russell Point Theater. You could predict the number of people in attendance almost any night of the week. June through August an influx of tourists helped a little. Most of them came to enjoy the lake, however, not to watch movies in an auditorium rancid with summer's heat.

The Russell Point theater wasn't making any financial headway, so Grandfather Tam and my father decided to make a change. So, they sold the theater and headed to Biloxi, Mississippi where they bought two theaters. Business was good in Biloxi during the temperate months, but although the gulf shoreline offered some respite in summer, July and August could be just as miserable as the temperature had been back in Ohio.

After a couple of years of no significant financial success, Grandpa heard about a water-cooled theater in Vallejo, California. Since business was no better in Biloxi than it had been at Russell Point, they decided to try their luck in California.

I was born in Vallejo, California on Tuesday, September 15, 1915. As my parents looked at me in the hospital room shortly after my birth, the doctor entered to fill out my birth certificate.

"Baby's name?" he asked.

"Stanley," my mother replied.

"Stanley?" my father rebutted. "I thought we decided on Stanford."

"You wanted Stanford," my mother said. "I always said it would be Stanley."

My parents entered into a dispute while the doctor waited patiently alongside. When he could at last get a word in edgewise, he said, "So what is it to be?"

"Make it John Doe," my mother answered, partly in disgust, partly facetious—which is what the doctor did. Several weeks later, it cost my dad $5 to go to the courthouse and have the name changed to Russell Stanley Tam.

Life and business were no better in Vallejo than they had been elsewhere. Grandfather Tam and my father sold the theater and we moved back to Ohio.

I wonder what my life would have been like had my father remained in the theater business. Doubtless I would have spent countless hours glued to a television set like many a typical kids today. Who knows? I might even have become an apprentice to my grandfather and his magic show, fashioning a career removed from those influences which were to so distinctly blueprint my future.

Yes, I could have lived out my years in the secular society with a secular career and little or no spiritual thought or pursuit. But in Jeremiah 29:11, speaking to the Hebrew exiles in Babylon, God laid down a principle that pertains to all of us: " 'For I know the plans I have for you,' declares the LORD, 'plans to prosper you and not to harm you, plans to give you hope and a future.' " And in Psalm 138:8: "The LORD will perfect that which concerneth me: thy mercy, O LORD, endureth for ever: forsake not the works of thine own hands" (KJV).

And, further, Isaiah 48:17-18: "I am the LORD your God, who teaches you what is best for you, who directs you in the way you should go. If only you had paid attention to my commands, your peace would have been like a river, your righteousness like the waves of the sea." What the Bible teaches is as plain: God is all-powerful and all-knowing. And above that, He is full of divine love and compassion. He created you and me for one sole purpose: that we might find and do His will for our lives.

Now I said, "What if" about my having remained in the initial vocation of my father and grandfather. The point is, I didn't. No, God had a plan for me, just as He has for you. He will mold circumstances to accommodate that plan. He will bring you, as you will subsequently see He brought me, into contact with people and events that form the framework for making His will and purpose known. Then it depends on us to choose to follow His guidance and to obey His mandates. We may only understand in a small way at first salvation, then commitment, the Holy Spirit's in-filling, then our obedience and initiative. It's such a beautiful plan! And God knew that, in my case, this plan would reach its fulfillment not in Biloxi, Mississippi, or in Vallejo, California, or any other place but in Lima, Ohio, in accordance with that rock steady promise in Romans 8:28, where the Bible says, "And we know that in all things God works for the good of those who love him, who have been called according to his purpose."

It may not happen all at once—it didn't for me—but in time you will learn of your need for faith. For me, once our family returned to Lima, Ohio I would in time face up to my need for faith in a God who not only saves a man's soul but, through that man's obedience, guides him into the discovery of a life abounding with faith, fruit and fulfillment.

THREE

I Could Have Become a Farmer

The good life down on the farm has produced its share of preachers, professional people and presidents. Something about the rural scene—the fertile soil, the fresh air, the wide horizons—has a positive effect on the life of a growing boy.

So it surely was with me.

After we returned from California, my father and grandfather spotted a "for sale" sign on a large farm immediately adjacent to the city limits of Lima. The land consisted of 174 acres, twenty of them woods, the remainder richly tillable.

"Let's buy it," my dad said.

"Using what for money?" his wife taunted, speaking with considerable authority. While our family moved around the country like restless vagabonds, pursuing one scheme after another, her father had become a wealthy landowner. He had made a fortune selling a large block of farm acres to a development group wishing to build a golf course and an amusement park. When he died, my mother received a substantial inheritance.

How he did it I never learned, but my father persuaded his frugal and domineering mate to use the money for a substantial down payment on the costly land.

The day we moved in, my father and mother stood on the veranda of our new home and looked out at the sprawling acres stirring in the breeze.

Grandfather Tam, being of an optimistic and practical mind, immediately struck on a lucrative plan for making use of all of that land. He quickly sold my parents on the idea of truck farming: taking the products of the farm—fresh produce, wood, etc.—into town to market directly to the townspeople.

Our farm's fertile acres produced 5,000 bushels of potatoes a year and over 500 bushels of soup beans. There were ripened-on-the-vine strawberries, big and sweet. We sold sweet corn, string beans, eggs, cabbage, plus peaches as big and succulent as those mouth-watering pictures on the covers of seed and nursery catalogs placed by the dozens in farmer's mailboxes from January through March.

With a horse-drawn bottom section farm wagon, my dad and I made twice-weekly trips into town. Housewives heard us coming and hurried out to their curbs with baskets. They proceeded to have us pile high freshly harvested delicacies. After a couple of tours, the Tam Truck Farm reputation spread widely.

Grandpa also set up a roadside stand just outside our farmyard gate, tended by my mother and sisters. My mother, being a woman of integrity, made scant effort to hide the fact she looked quite positively at the farm's fulfilling of Grandpa Tam's prognostications as to its potential.

Although a young boy, I about decided to forfeit all my dreams and become a farmer!

* * *

As sisters go, mine—Evelyn, two years older than I, Mildred, two years younger (we called her Midge)—were OK. I didn't care all that much for their dolls and their playhouses, but I liked the way each could swing a baseball bat and run in a game of tag or scamper up into the farm's hayloft. I especially approved of the expertise with which either of them could spread peanut butter, embellished with honey, onto a slice of thick homemade bread, doing it for the nurture and good will of a hungry brother.

Apart from the farm's own appealing aspects, the skies above it provided a special and spectacular wonderment. Less than a hundred miles separated Lima from Dayton. Dayton had become the hub of the "aeroplane world" in those days—it being the site where the Wright Brothers transformed bicycles into flying machines. Thus, until the advent of larger passenger planes, Dayton remained pretty much the center for aircraft construction, experimentation and demonstration. So it was a common event to be outdoors on the farm and hear the drone of approaching aircraft. On such occasions, the men in the fields and the women in the houses and all personnel in between positioned themselves for a look skyward at the approaching wonder.

* * *

Evelyn and Midge devoted a large part of their time to helping mother in the house. So, not having a brother, I was often left to my own devices for outdoor activities. Of course, as I grew older, I was expected to help with farm activities and responsibilities.

I didn't mind working with my father and grandfather. Although they never said it in words, by nonverbal actions and attitudes they showed their affection and appreciation for me.

My dad usually took me with him on his route peddling vegetables around the residential area. He wanted me mostly for company, I'm sure, but I soon learned to bag up orders with expertise.

In those days, prior to the advent of supermarkets, small neighborhood grocery stores proliferated, making it a simple matter for my father to pass by one of them and stop while I ran in to purchase a Baby Ruth candy bar—my favorite—as a reward for services rendered.

Going with my dad from house to house did wonders for my diffident personality. When city boys appeared and looked at me as someone they could give a rough time, I had the security of the wagon and the presence of my father to help me overcome my shyness and, though I never challenged any of them, to feel comfortably secure. Of course, many other boys were friendly. One in particular would bring out a ball from his house and, as my father chatted with his mother and made up her order, the two of us would play toss and catch.

Since our farm was so near, boys who had become friendly with me often came to visit. They looked upon me—or at least I thought they did—as someone of importance due to my being involved in the sales routes and living on a farm with its intriguing diversions.

The town vegetable routes only lasted for a short period each summer, and I spent most of my time on the farm itself.

I can't say I enjoyed working in the fields. Putting up hay and arranging bundles of oats and barley into shocks prior to the arrival of the threshing machine all added up to hard work. Farms today are like industrial plants, with well-designed implements to work the land, huge tractors and combines harvesting the output of the soil. We did everything either by horse power or by human power. We milked a lot of cows, for example, not with machines but by hand. I looked longingly, many times, at the advertisements for milking machines which appeared in farm magazines.

* * *

Living close to town the way we did, we had lots of visitors. Often, when relatives came, we would picnic in the yard. My mother frequently made hand-cranked ice cream. We had a big freezer, and unless the number of visitors was exceptionally large, I could eat ice cream until my frosted throat refused another swallow.

My favorite visitor was always my cousin Bud, who lived in town but loved our farm so fervently he came out to see us whenever he could. Sometimes he would come for a couple of days or for a whole week, and I in turn would visit him at his house in town.

There were four McBeth wives in all and, in the process of time, one of them—Bud's mother—got converted and began attending the Alliance Church. Bud's father never became a believer. Of all our relatives, we were closest to Bud's family.

Mostly Bud came to see me alone, which I preferred, but occasionally he brought a friend or two from town, or kids from our larger family circle came. Our barn held special attraction for all young visitors. We had a great time in the sweet-smelling hay playing hide-and-seek or cops and robbers.

*   *   *

I joined the FFA (Future Farmers of America), selected a newborn gilt—a female pig, that is—and raised her to maturity. Some don't realize a pig can become as good a friend to a boy as a dog or a cat.

The FFA program was part of our school curriculum, and I was given specific instructions on feed and care. As a result, my female hog presented me with a litter of eight hearty piglets. I sold her and her brood and after deducting food and expenses, cleared $25, sufficient capitalization to make possible the cash purchase of a state-of-the-art Sears bicycle. I loved that bike, rode it so much my mother had difficulty bringing me to terms with work she wanted done. For example, mowing lawn grass surrounding the house. You might say we had one of the earliest Lawn-Boy mowers—that is to say, I was the lawn boy!

Perhaps you can envision one of those antique units where the person pushing provides power. Even in the best of conditions, such a lawnmower rapidly consumed human energy. If the mower was not properly sharpened or was out of adjustment, pushing became a mighty chore indeed. So I avoided the task whenever I could.

But one day my mother slipped up on me and—grabbing the handlebars of my bicycle—looked full into my face to say, "Stanley, if you don't get that grass mowed today, it will be so long it can't be cut."

I, of course, hadn't told her that was my delay tactic all along!

Even though it was midafternoon, a long time since breakfast, she said, "You get after that lawn, Stanley, and when you're finished, I'll fix you all the pancakes you can eat."

As she well knew, pancakes rated with me on a par with candy and ice cream. Four hours later, the job done, when I entered the house as hungry as I was exhausted, she already had the dough mixed and the frying pan sizzling atop the stove.

The rules of the game were that she would literally fix all I could eat, no questions asked. My goal was twenty, but the last bite of the eighteenth pancake had to be washed down with a couple gulps of water.

My mother may not have been a gourmet cook but she had a reputation for expertise in bringing out the best from such staples as meat, potatoes and . . . well . . . pancakes.

Reputation, did I say?

It's time I told you that the Erie Railroad ran adjacent to our farm along one boundary. It seemed hardly a day passed but what one knight of the road, as hoboes were called, hopped off a slow-moving freight train and came up to our house to ask my mother for a meal. She never turned one of them down. Both my father and mother advised against my engaging in conversation with any of these drifters. But I would sit and watch them. They didn't know where their next meal would come from or where they would sleep the coming night. The hoboes heightened my determination to make a success of my life.

The farm prospered. Although the mortgage remained heavy, due to the amount of acreage, my father and grandfather became known as the wealthiest men in our extended family. No boy had more packages with his name on them under the Christmas tree than I did each Yule Season.

* * *

Prosperous we truly were. The truck farming income increased with each passing year. The county commissioner approached my father and grandfather about purchasing our farm because it was an ideal location for an airport. Without hesitation they refused.

But then came 1929 and the big crash.

The depression hovered over America like a plague. The bottom dropped out of the market. Banks closed. People lost their jobs. Our farm, still under mortgage, was in danger of foreclosure.

My mother turned on my father like a wounded animal turns on the person coming to its aid. "Why did I ever listen to you?" she lamented. "All the money you spent on silly tools and machines you didn't need, money that could have finished off the mortgage."

It got so they quarreled constantly, during the day and on into the night. Many of the nights during warm weather I would go out and sleep by a corn shock or nest with a pet pig to get away from the loud tirades that often continued beyond the midnight hour.

My father soon gave up any defense and would stand in silent meekness as my mother lambasted him. I overheard them several times speak of divorce, and I'm sure they would have if it were not for us three children.

My father tried a wide variety of schemes to make money, from opening a golf driving range to washing the emulsion from photographic film and selling the clear plastic, but each attempt failed.

My father very nearly died of a broken heart. My mother was forced to partner with a neighbor lady to do family washings for twenty-five cents a bundle so she could finish putting us kids through high school. The two women would do as many as ten washings per day.

* * *

In all of this recounting, I have not mentioned my spiritual life.

I profited much by living on the farm. But I needed more. Sunday church services continued in the four-room schoolhouse. It was a good group. The various pastors did not oppose the gospel but neither did they preach it. Yet I did assimilate enough in the Sunday school lessons and the preaching to begin sensing an emptiness in my heart.

As I think back, I wonder. *What if I had had a Sunday school teacher who really cared about my spiritual needs? What if I could have been involved in something like Boys Brigade or Youth for Christ with their emphasis on helping young people make Christ the focal point of their lives?*

Those questions always bring me around to thoughts of children today. Is there a child in your Sunday school, a young person in your youth society, who would respond to encouragement, loving attention and concern? Please take the time to reach out to that child—it could make all the difference in his life.

My First Cigarette—and Last

During a high school outing to the Ohio State campus, I was presented with my first opportunity to try a cigarette.

My associate gestured toward a bench along the sidewalk, walked over toward it and sat down. I joined him. He was obviously pretending to be a collegian, as he reached into his shirt pocket and took out an unopened pack of Camel cigarettes.

"Like a cigarette?" he asked as he proceeded to open the package.

"As a matter of fact, I would," I told him. "I've been wanting to try a cigarette for a long time."

When he had the pack opened, he gave a slight tap and one came popping out. "Here," he said, holding the pack over to me. "Be my guest."

I took the cigarette, looked at it a moment and then put it in my mouth. Meanwhile, my friend opened a book of matches, struck one and held the light over to me.

"Oh," I said, holding up a hand in restraint, "I don't want to smoke it. I've just been curious to find out what it's like to have a cigarette in your mouth."

"You a coward?" he scoffed. "You've got to light it and puff on it to know what it's like."

When I continued to refrain as he held the match closer, he grabbed the cigarette and put it into his own mouth, lit it and then sat puffing on it like Mr. Big Man in person. Although anti-smoking campaigns lay yet several decades into the future, I knew something of the perils of tobacco.

"My dad told me about people he knew who died of lung cancer," I said.

"Lung cancer?" my companion scoffed, blowing a long puff into the air. "How does anybody livin' on the farm like us guys do, with all that fresh air an stuff, how're we gonna get lung cancer?"

Those moments on the Ohio State Campus became a decisive event in my life. I could have permitted my friend to light that cigarette. Knowing me, I probably would have choked on the first puff. On the other hand, I might have liked it. I could have taken to the habit. With me, it wasn't so much a matter of willpower as it was "won't power."

And, as years passed, my total abstinence from both smoking and drinking added a distinct strength to the building of my character. That weekend on the Ohio State Campus attended by members of our agricultural class in high school also had a distinct effect upon me. Speakers to whom we listened made farming by modern methods an attractive option to young boys such as myself considering their future vocations.

One speaker especially had a kind of abounding personality that made you believe everything he said. "Don't get caught up in this present phobia which causes young people, born on the farm, to seek their livelihood in the city," he said. "Just remember that the more population decreases on the farm, the wider become your opportunities for success as farmers."

Well, of one thing I was sure. I did not want to be a farmer. I had learned from close observation that farming is not the way to get rich, and one driving force motivated the life of young Stanley Tam, and that was the determination to make money—lots of money. But how?

I observed that professional people—doctors, attorneys, etc.—made money. I ruled myself out on such potentials, however, realizing the many years of education that would be required. I thought of trying my hand at inventing, but soon realized I had more of a mechanical mind than an inventor's intellect.

The only potential that came to my thoughts was that of salesmanship. I once heard someone speak of "buy low, sell high" as the prevailing rule for success in selling. I could lie in bed at night, for instance, imagining myself a salesman, and fall asleep and dream of boldly approaching potential clients, convincing them to purchase my products. But then, upon awakening, I would always come back to the question of how I could ever bring myself to approach a stranger, to introduce myself and my product and make a sale.

Searching through a scrap heap one afternoon, I found a couple of discarded bicycle frames and parts. These I took home and began my exciting new enterprise. When I ran out of scrap heaps as a resource, I paid boys twenty five cents for used parts they could find in their neighborhoods. A wheel from one reject, handle bars from another, any usable seat from a third and in one day's time I could assemble a good unit.

These reclaimed bikes became especially saleable when I painted them. My father taught me how to include decorative stripes. When finished, even to my critical eye, it was as though some of those salvaged two-wheelers had ridden off the pages of a Sears & Roebuck Catalog.

The reclaimed bikes became overnight sensations. Word of mouth did my advertising. I had occasional delusions of grandeur, in which I imagined Tam Manufacturing Corporation, builders of the finest in low-cost bicycles.

I began to have some extra money in my pocket. Believe me, one thing Stanley Tam learned to appreciate in those earliest days of merchandising experience was the sheer pleasure of making money. In that manner, those reclaimed bicycles played a significant role in my life.

Enthusiasm for reclaimed bicycles wore thin for the simple reason I had increasing difficulty obtaining parts. I began looking for more stable sales or manufacturing options. I had often browsed through farm catalogs, noticing how many of the advertisements involved stocking product at a low price and then selling it at a profitable margin.

I didn't relish the idea of ringing doorbells over against waiting for customers to come on their own, as with my reclaimed bicycles. Then, too, I was smart enough to know you couldn't simply paint a sign—attractive as such a sign might be with my past experience—and expect customers to come to me.

The year 1929 brought with it the nation-staggering bank holiday imposed by President Franklin D. Roosevelt, a bold—and at the time, frightening—effort to stem depression economics. Banks had been closing in epidemic proportions, causing customers to loose their savings and deposits.

I remember my parents discussing that they had lost what money they had when, as banks cautiously reopened, under government supervision, depositors were paid ten cents on the dollar.

Suicides were rampant, and the mood across the country was one of defeat and despair.

My father subsequently lost the farm and we had to move into town, where we rented a house from a former wealthy real estate developer who literally went insane from depression stress.

* * *

As depression woes worsened, my father took a job selling coal to suppliers such as fuel depots and lumber yards. I sometimes accompanied him and marveled at his ability to make a certain brand of coal appealing to the potential customer.

I ordered a supply of salve from one of the farm magazine advertisements which assured it could cure everything from warts, ringworm, acne, pimples, as well as headaches. When the shipment arrived, I carried it with trembling hands to my room, opened the box and familiarized myself with the salve.

But as I tried to imagine myself taking a small jar of salve, for example, and describing it with sufficient authority to cause a housewife to make a purchase, I cringed with apprehension. Yet door to door I went, sometimes getting only as far as the veranda when, reaching out to touch the doorbell, my courage vanished and I hotfooted it back to the sidewalk.

Most of the women shook their heads and motioned for me to go on my way. I would have given up, but a few made purchases and I kept going.

A formula for successful selling, I had been told, is to make ten calls and expect at least one sale out of each ten. In my case, I realized I was making closer to fifteen for each sale.

Going to my room one night, I dumped the paltry collection of coins from the day's sales onto my bed counting just over $1 for the day's total effort. Sometimes sales added up to scarcely a dollar—a far cry from the great days of selling reclaimed bicycles.

Discouragement gnawed at me, and I wondered if I would ever make anything of myself. Did I even have sufficient talent to try?

President Roosevelt instituted such things as the WPA (Works Progress Administration), which provided work plus surplus foods for thousands across the country. Pay was upper poverty scale at best. I was much too young to qualify, and my father was much too proud to accept such a handout.

Often at night, I lay in bed unable to sleep, wondering how I could ever possibly make any kind of success in life. What a difference it might have made if I had had some kind of Christian influence! At that time I knew so little about spiritual things, I couldn't even form spiritual thoughts, much less cause myself to wonder about such a thing as Christian influence.

I did remember, however, how years earlier I had gone out in the dark to bring in the cattle for a late milking. It happened that some of them were grazing at the farthest corner of the pasture, so I had a long walk.

As the last of the cows began heading back to the barn, a beautiful moon arose. I loved the moon and the stars, and could even name a number of the constellations. I especially enjoyed a full moon, cherishing those moments when the night sentinel first edged up from the horizon like a bright ember of the sun itself.

"Where are You, God?" I whispered aloud. "I would like to know You."

It was a solemn moment, this first attempt at intercession. How very far removed I was in those moments from the day when prayer would become a priority of my life. At this time in my childhood, however, I thought of prayer as something you did only at church. Thus all the more significant became my effort to talk to God that evening in the pasture.

Frankly, I was so unschooled and inexperienced in spiritual matters in those days, I scarcely recognized the very solid fact that the restlessness and emptiness I felt in my life stemmed directly from my need to talk to God and, from the Bible, have Him converse with me.

FIVE

Depression Scars

The depression made an impact upon my life I could never erase, even though I have been privileged to make substantial amounts of money. To this day I am not comfortable sitting in a luxury hotel or going to an expensive restaurant.

Our mother and father could not give us spending money allowances other than a nickel or a dime for some special occasion. Many times I went in to confectionaries and wondered what a green river soda tasted like. I watched a man order a thick chocolate milk shake he could only consume with a spoon. In those days you could buy a penny's worth of candy, and I remember having a nickel in my pocket and the pleasure it gave me to purchase three sticks of licorice, one for each of my sisters and one for myself, then investing the remaining two pennies for as many sticks of gum.

Since those days, I have often had days when our company banked over $100,000. I would not waste one of those dollars, much less expend five or ten of them on some trivial or selfish purchase.

Yet I am by no stretch of the definition a miser. I wear good clothing, drive a late model automobile, live in a comfortable home. It's just that, through the years, I have been unable—not that I have especially tried—to erase the memory of 1929 when, during my freshman year in high school, the depression began. I remember my father and mother sitting at the kitchen table staring straight ahead, stunned. My mother practically blamed my father for the entire national plight and harangued him incessantly about the large mortgage yet remaining on the property.

"We could have paid it," she fumed, "but we can't now. We'll lose the farm. You watch and see." This would go on and on until my father, stumbling to his feet, went outside.

The previous year, a tax assessment had been made against our property to finance substantial improvements on the highway alongside our land. The contractor went bankrupt and the highway was closed for several years.

Even though he steered clear of his wife's tirades whenever possible, my dad was willing to take all the blame. He tried desperately to stem the tide of economic catastrophe, but it was like telling the sun not to rise in the morning or set at the close of the day.

Let me say something about the fairness of my parents during those difficult times. I continued to play away at my sales efforts, trying to push one product and then another and hoarding what I earned. They could so easily have commanded me to turn over all my earnings to help bolster the family budget, but they didn't.

One time my mother came into my room when I was sprawled out on my bed sorting coins. I had a dollar or more on display. At the sight of my mother, I possessively scooped the coins toward myself.

"Silly boy!" she scoffed. "Do you suppose I would touch a nickel of your money? What do you take me for?" If my mother had turned on me and demeaned me for my inabilities as a salesman, I don't know what I would have done.

Sometimes I stood at the door to our house and looked out at the horizon and, without thinking, poise myself to dash forward and run and run until I somehow broke free forever from the lingering bondage of my childhood.

Emptiness grew in my heart. At first, I assessed it to be economic circumstances. But I had heard enough through years of Sunday school to realize every human being had a desire to know God. I knew nothing of Him, beyond the three letters in His name, and I never read the Bible, knew little if any Scripture other than the Lord's Prayer, John 3:16 and Psalm 23. I was spiritually illiterate.

Shy though I was, and prone to discouragement, I continued ringing doorbells.

"Sonny boy," I would hear, "how can I buy any of your products, not one of which I have the slightest need, when I'm duty bound to spread a table for my family three times a day?" Or, "If I was to buy one of those little doodads of yours, it would be the same as you stealing money from me. Now get along. Don't waste my time."

Customer after customer, that was the story. I almost sighed with relief when I would ring a doorbell and find no one at home. Worse than that, I stepped onto many a front veranda on the streets of Lima only to reach out for the doorbell and then withdraw my hand, so shy I was, so sure of failure in my efforts.

But I did make sales. Night after night, stretched out on my bed, I watched in muted wonder as my meager wealth increased.

* * *

Like many boys in those times I became intrigued with automobiles. In spite of the depression, there were men who could afford to purchase one. Such an array of them there were: Durant, Buick, Oldsmobile, Cadillac, Hupmobile, Studebaker, to begin a list. Then there were the standards, Chevrolet and Ford.

Underscoring all these makes and models was the incredible Model T, the genius of Henry Ford. Mr. Ford determined to manufacture an automobile the common man could afford to purchase and drive. I was personally challenged by the story of how he did it, how he faced obstacle upon obstacle as he endeavored to produce a vehicle both efficient and economical.

Henry Ford and the Model T Ford inadvertently challenged me to somehow overcome my belief that I could never make it as a salesman. It also caught my eye as an object of desire.

How I did it, I don't really know, but night after night and week after week, month after month, as I counted earnings in my room, the total increased. Then, I learned about a used Model T available for the amazing price of $15. Prosperity was in the bountiful countryside, not along languishing city streets, I had been told. With the prestige and convenience of an automobile, Stanley Tam could become a successful salesman at last. I was convinced of it. And so, with stars in my eyes, I negotiated the purchase of that Model T Ford.

SIX

Model T Mania

The world became a friendlier place with the purchase of that used Model T.

The ingenious Henry Ford had not only created an automobile most people could own, he had also designed it so it was as simple to drive as a bicycle.

When I went to pick up my first vehicle, I found it in need of some tender loving care. At first, it took several moments to get the motor running, but with a bit of mechanical help from my cousin Bud, we got the motor back into better condition. Initially hard to start, it became shipshape. Driving it took only rudimentary dexterity and elemental intelligence.

I had myself an automobile!

The amazingly simplistic Model T had two levers on its steering gear—one for spark, one for throttle. It had no battery, only a profoundly efficient magneto. You gave your engine lots of spark when initially turning the crank, which was located just below the front radiator. Once the motor started, you rushed back to the steering wheel and adjusted the spark. Failing to do so incited a Fourth of July simulation of bangs and pops spewing outward from the tailpipe. How I did love that sound!

Model T efficiency was matched by its simplicity. My cousin and I became overnight mechanics. We took the engine apart, every piece of it. "All this thing needs is to be cleaned up," Bud said.

"We've got to get rid of as much of that rust as we can," I added.

We soon had it running like a full-fledged Cadillac! It was a thrill to drive down the street, adjusting the spark until your car sounded more like an artillery gun at a battlefield than a motorized human conveyance. I learned that too much spark could be disastrous to a Model T's ignition system so, with rare exceptions, I tempered my playfulness.

I loved to drop by my cousin Bud's house. He would hear me approaching in the distance and would be standing waiting for me. He was adept at jumping into the car without bothering to open a door.

Speed limits and traffic cops were nonexistent in those days. Indeed, most cars did not function well at high speeds. The Model T certainly did not. But I did often urge top performance out of my pride and joy, so that we created quite a spectacle churning along the streets of Lima.

The Model T gave a boost to my ego those days. Sitting at the wheel, honking my horn, waving at acquaintances along the street, sometimes I felt as though I didn't have a shy bone in my body. The Model T also enhanced my status with the girls, and Bud and I would take our friends on rides around the area. Bud, who could be much more overt in social encounters than was I, had a steady girlfriend. Made bold by the increase in my popularity thanks to the Model T, I somehow roused sufficient courage to approach a girl to whom I had long taken a fancy. I'm sure she might have rejected me in the past, but the Model T made the difference. She, Bud, his girlfriend and I had great times cruising around Lima. Of course, my prime intent in the use of the Model T was for sales out in the rural area where I had convinced myself I would find customers more lenient. The mere sight and sound of an automobile coming into a farmyard, it seemed to me, would enhance receptivity to my products.

I can never forget that balmy spring day when I first ventured out onto country roads. I'd been able to secure a franchise for products, some fifty items such as extracts, tea mixes, puddings, toothbrushes, bathroom powders, soaps and sundry choices. I also found a wholesale outlet for such items as shoe strings, shoe polish, gargles, aspirin, iodine, bandages, plus pins and needles, which brought my total up to one hundred items in all.

I hired three boys to make door-to-door calls in Lima, leaving me free to explore the countryside. Stanley Tam, the young entrepreneur, was on the move. Success was just a matter of time.

I had brushed up on my sales technique too. For example, I had read an article about how people like to hear their names spoken, so when I came to a farm prospect, I took care to read the name on the mailbox. That worked OK until I came to a place where the former attendant Mr. Jones, whose name was on the mailbox, had moved away and the farm was now tilled by a Mr. Smith.

Many farmers, even though congenial, were as sales resistant as the townsfolk. Their wives were especially resistant to my sales pitch. More than once I would have the man of the place about ready to buy then he would say, "First I'd better talk to the missus and see what she thinks." And often that meant I could just as well start up and drive away.

But I did make a few sales, slightly exceeding what I earned in town. I was able to take care of all my own expenses, purchasing clothes, paying a couple of dollars for board and room at home, and mostly I had my car to enjoy, often taking it on leisurely drives around Lima.

Bud was always ready for a ride. I needed only to pull up to his house and he would come bounding out the door and into the Model T. One day as we drove leisurely along, Bud spotted an older lady up ahead carrying a cumbersome bag of groceries.

"That's my aunt," he said, pointing.

"Let's give her a lift," I suggested.

"Not sure you'd want to. All she talks is hell, fire and brimstone." Carefully noting what my cousin had said, I pulled up to the curb. Out of curiosity the woman stopped.

Bud glanced at me. I didn't quite understand the expression in his eyes. I just nodded my head and gestured toward the lady.

With a you-asked-for-it look in his eye, Bud called out, "Come on board, Aunt Magie," he invited. "We'll take you home. No charge, huh, Stanley?"

"All rides free on Saturdays," I said amiably.

Aunt Magie was about to turn and continue walking but Bud bounded from the car, swooped the grocery bag out of her arms and carried it back to the Model T. "Come on, Aunt Magie," he urged, "Stanley's a good driver."

Reluctantly, with a bit more urging, Aunt Magie got into the car. "OK," Bud called out.

When his aunt was seated in the back and Bud had resumed his place beside me he muttered, "Let 'er rip." Summoning my car to give peak performance, I complied. We headed down the street like the last stretch of a roller coaster ride.

"Take it easy there, young man," the passenger called out.

"Scare her good," my cousin muttered to me. "She needs it."

But even to the faintest of hearts, the piddling speed of a Model T became quickly commonplace, and soon the elderly lady regained composure. "What kind of devilment are you up to?" she wanted to know. "You got nothing better to do than go gallivanting around like this?"

"We ain't up to nothin'," Bud told her. "We was just drivin'."

"The Lord help us," she broke in. "I don't know what things is a comin' to. You runnin' off to dances, playin' cards, goin' to the movies. Likely you two just came from the pool room, didn't you?"

"No, Auntie," Bud replied.

"You're both on the road straight to hell," she continued. "We're having prayer meeting in church tonight. If you had an ounce of sense, you'd be there and get yourselves saved."

When we reached her house, Bud scurried around to open her door, but she sat resolute and continued thundering preachments at us. Finally, her sermon completed, she permitted her nephew to take the grocery bag and carry it to her house.

"I do pray for your lost soul, son," she intoned as she left the Model T and headed toward her domicile.

As we drove away Bud apologized, saying, "You sorry you suggested we pick her up?"

"Nah, that's OK," I told him. "Always glad to help."

"My dad says when she dies and goes to heaven, she'll try to boss God the same as she does people down here on earth."

Actually, the crabby old woman got through to me just a little bit, causing me to face the fact that I didn't have a clue about what it took to go to heaven.

For sure, my trusty Model T was opening new experiences for me.

The Greatest of All Miracles

I tried to convince myself that, having graduated from high school, it would only be a matter of time until I came upon some sales scheme which would give me the success I so longed for. I responded to one newspaper ad by ordering twenty-four boxes of candy together with a punch board. Buy a box of candy and you qualified for one punch which, for lucky clients, involved receiving a second box of candy free. People liked the idea and it only took a few days until I had sold all the boxes, netting me an attractive markup. The problem, however, was that, when my friends learned about the money I had made, I became deluged with requests to borrow.

"I'll pay you back double," one said, with the end result that he didn't pay me back anything. Only two or three repaid. Others acknowledged owing me but, assuming my affluence gave them license to delay payment, they also kept my money. My soft-heartedness made a failure out of success.

Next, I came upon a magazine promotional with the heading: Make Yourself a Fragrant Fortune! I responded and received a quantity of the product which was claimed to be a perfume directly imported from Paris and, at the bargain price offered, sure to charm any woman who considered it. I hit the sidewalk on door-to-door selling once again. Sales resistance matched anything I had previously tried.

The perfume smelled OK to me, but when others took a whiff, they wrinkled their noses in rejection.

One husband came to the door, took the bottle from his wife and held it to his nose, then exclaimed, "What is this—essence of polecat?"

I gave up in massive discouragement. Not only did I lose the income I had anticipated, I was stuck with the unsold merchandise.

It was about this time something happened which could have made a substantial difference to my spiritual status. Bud's family regularly attended church and, in his early high school years, my cousin abruptly professed conversion. He became so sincere in his new spiritual identity, he made a special trip to our farm to tell me about it and the great feelings he was having.

"Wouldn't you like that same feeling?" he asked me.

"Well, I guess I would," I replied.

"OK," he responded, "let's ride into town next Sunday night and you can get saved same as I did."

Early afternoon on the following Lord's Day, Bud arrived on his bicycle. We played a bit, as though nothing had happened, but immediately after the evening meal, my cousin made sure we headed into town. Like two medieval knights we were, resolutely setting out to find the Holy Grail.

We arrived early. However, instead of taking a customary seat at the back, Bud suggested we move all the way down to the front.

"That will make it easier for you," he said. "Tell you what I'll do. When it's time for you to go forward and get saved, I'll let you know, OK?"

"OK," I replied dubiously. I became uneasy, sitting there at the very front of the church. But Bud's enthusiasm was contagious.

The entire sermon could best be described as a continuous peal of thunder, the evangelist raising his voice to a judicial frenzy and keeping it there for well over an hour. It was the first time I had heard hell, fire and brimstone proclaimed as an option for the end of a person's life, and I became gripped by an emotion I had not before experienced.

From what Bud had told me about his own experience, I presumed the same option would be offered to me. I can't say I looked forward to it, but I didn't feel strongly resistant to it either.

As the evangelist concluded his sermon, however, he switched subject matter from the fires of hell to the power whereby God could heal the sick, open blind eyes and unstop deaf ears. Then he gave an invitation to those who wanted to be healed. Several went forward. There was no mention of salvation.

"Maybe he gets to the salvation part later," Bud whispered.

I grew restless, as did Bud.

The two of us lingered until after the benediction. People vacated the auditorium, leaving us sitting awkwardly in a pew by ourselves. Except that I had not been presented with an opportunity to make any response, the event replicated an earlier experience that I had had at the country school house.

Bud invited me to attend youth meetings at the church. I was pleased to go any place where I could drive up in my Model T and have people notice. But I also found the meetings themselves to my liking. The young people had a happy spirit, seemed to genuinely enjoy their Christianity about which they spoke with obvious enthusiasm, something new in my experience.

* * *

I decided if I couldn't overcome my shyness and face people with poise and conviction, I could never succeed. I spent hours in my room pretending to sell the products I handled to imaginary customers.

Actually, I became quite proficient. At times I was able to leave the house brimming with optimism and determination. When I drove my Model T into a farmyard, however, the old bugaboo reared its head. I trembled and began to sweat.

One morning, as I drove off into new territory, the specter of defeat came over me. I didn't have the courage to turn into a farmyard, much less go to the door and attempt a sale. I passed farmhouse after farmhouse, sometimes slowing down, sometimes almost turning in.

"Look, Stanley," I spoke aloud, "you've got to get over this foolishness." I turned into the very next farmstead. There was nobody home. I felt like calling it a day.

I was on a dirt road with deep ruts, making travel precarious, otherwise I would have driven at a brisk rate back toward Lima. As it was, I proceeded so slowly it seemed equally awkward to pass by a farm driveway than to turn in. Approaching one place, I noted both a man and woman working in a small garden near the house.

With a sheer burst of boldness, I turned in.

"I see he handles the Zanol brand," the wife said. "There was a woman visiting our circle last week from over by Findlay. She talked right out about Zanol. She said it's the best she ever used."

"How much is your vanilla?" the husband asked me.

"Thirty-nine cents a bottle," I answered, my shyness sublimated for the moment by their attitude.

"Land sakes," the wife responded. "We can get it for ten cents a bottle in at the store."

"But you'll find that's imitation vanilla, ma'am," I said. "The Zanol vanilla is pure extract, not diluted in any way."

I saw both of them stiffen at my argument.

"What kind of puddings are those?" the man asked.

"Only the best," I answered.

The man chuckled, winked at his wife, then turned to me and said, "What else do they tell you to say?" My spirits waned. I could see the sale slipping out of my hands.

"Let me be real honest with you, son," the man continued. "Everywhere you go, I'm sure people tell you how tight money is. Well, it is. We haven't took our eggs and cream to town yet this week, so we're real short on change. You come this way later in the week, and maybe we'll buy something. I ain't promisin' though."

It was the worst morning I'd had in weeks, and I about decided that if I had at that moment been in Lima and someone offered me a job in a filling station at $5 a week, I would have taken it without hesitation.

The road became increasingly rutted, accurately fitting my mood but also bringing down my speed to such a crawl I got a detailed view of an approaching farmyard. Buildings freshly painted. Lawn mowed. Flowers surrounded the house and there were added touches of color elsewhere.

On the mailbox I saw the name George Long. Something about that short name sounded friendly and so, although reluctantly, I turned into the yard, drove up to a point near the house and stopped.

It was October 15, 1933, and would become one of the mile marker days in my life.

I waited in the car a moment, always taking special note of the nature of a farmer's dog. Then too I thought I might see someone so I wouldn't need to go into the often negative confines of a house. You were never so much at the behest of a potential customer, it seemed to me, as when you entered his residence.

But no one came, neither man nor dog, so I ventured out of the vehicle, and moved reluctantly toward the house. For some reason, I felt a magnetic pull that quickened my pace. In retrospect, as you will understand, I now know why I became so disposed. Even when I reached the door, my usual reluctance gave away to some kind of optimism by which I was able to promptly knock. The door opened much sooner than would normally be the case. There stood a young woman with as friendly a face as I had seen in a month of door openings.

"Uh, Mrs. Long," I blurted, remembering the name on the mailbox, "my name is Stanley Tam. I represent Zanol Products, the finest line of household and kitchen items available these days."

"My," Mrs. Long exclaimed, "aren't you quite the salesman? And such a young man. You must be just a beginner."

"Yes, ma'am," I managed to respond, not quite sure what my reaction should be to her engaging—or was it demeaning?—welcome.

Stepping back and gesturing to the interior of her house, she said, "Please come in. Like farm folks you meet wherever you go, I suppose, money is as scarce as hen's teeth around this place. How do you find selling? Everybody short on money?" I nodded. "Well, let's see what you have in that crafty display case of yours."

She gestured for me to put the case on the table, which I did, opening it. In that moment, I noticed a Bible over to one side.

"You certainly keep a neat display," she commented.

"Thank you, ma'am."

"Oh, Zanol products! I've heard other ladies talk about their good quality!"

I put out condiments, basic medicines, combs, brushes and the like. I had never encountered such a customer before. Mrs. Long, a woman in her thirties, was short and chubby with a happy, effervescent personality. I became absolutely certain she was going to purchase a substantial number of items. In fact, she egged me on as I talked about the Zanol products and other items I had for sale.

Finally, she said, "I need to tell you that my husband and I don't own this farm. We aren't even renters. George receives $8 a week to look after the crops and harvest and all. So money is as scarce as can be. Doubtless, that's your experience as well. It keeps a body figuring to put food on the table."

My spirits ebbed.

"You made an excellent presentation," she continued. "You certainly have talent."

"We won't need to worry about money much longer," I said, "President Roosevelt has a great program going. He'll have us out of this depression in a few months."

"Do you think so?" she asked.

"I'm sure of it. Take the NRA program, for example."

This led us into a brief political discussion. Then, seeing I was not likely to make any further progress, I prepared to leave.

"Please don't go," she urged. "I gave you time to tell me about the things you have to sell. Now maybe you would be willing to listen to my presentation."

Not having a clue what she was up to, I felt somewhat bewildered.

"You are a talented young man," she told me, warmth evident in her voice. "You will make your mark in the world. But no matter how successful you become, even if you acquire a great amount of wealth, you will always be striving for something more. Never satisfied. Not until you settle the most important question in the world."

"What is that?" I asked.

She smiled and said, "Your relationship with God."

"Oh," I stammered. "I attend church. I never use profanity or things like that. I've never smoked, never touched alcohol. I have a reputation for living a clean life."

"But do you know Jesus Christ as your personal Savior?" She spoke so gently, with such a keen concern for me as a person, I couldn't protest. She picked up her Bible and, for the next two hours, gave me a detailed presentation of why every person on earth needs salvation and what God has done through Christ to provide that salvation. She told me how empty her life had been and how she had tried to find satisfaction and a purpose for living.

"My situation was perhaps somewhat similar to your own," she said, "I was such a good person, even religious you might say, that I didn't see why I needed salvation. I thought being lost meant you were guilty of many bad sins.

"To be lost means you are not in a relationship with God. You are not a member of His family. When you are born again, you become a member of God's family." She told me of answers to prayer in her life, of times when the Lord lifted her out of confusion and discouragement into peace and fulfillment. Using her Bible, she introduced me to the plan of salvation. Turning to the third chapter of Romans, she showed me the verse, "All have sinned and fall short of the glory of God" (3:23). Then in chapter six, "For the wages of sin is death, but the gift of God is eternal life in Jesus Christ our Lord" (6:23). Turning the pages, she pointed out Romans 10:13: "For whosoever shall call upon the name of the Lord shall be saved" (KJV).

For the first time in my life I felt the awesome impact of Scripture. It would happen again, many times, without ever becoming commonplace.

Commonplace? Yes, a good checkup on your spiritual life can be made by simply noting your response to the reading or hearing of the Bible. If the Bible, heard or read, does not touch your inner spirit, you need to do a checkup.

I presumed she would be taking the matter of those salvation verses farther. She didn't, because at that moment a car drove into their yard, some relatives dropping by for a surprise visit. "Do come back again, Mr. Tam," she said. "I'll try to be a better customer next time."

I had mixed emotions as I left Mrs. Long's kitchen, wanting to get away from the dynamic and persuasive woman but, at the same time, realizing that the fulfillment for which I had so long searched could be found by putting into action, in my own life, the impact of her witness.

The Mrs. Long kind of person was supposed to be a religious fanatic, like Bud's Aunt Magie, in my glossary of definitions. But she wasn't. She was radiant and genuine, compelling without offensive pressure. I was convinced she had spiritual reality, the kind for which I was searching.

Driving away from the Long farm that morning, I tried to make a deal with God, to come to terms with Him. Of course, I wanted those terms to be my terms. I would accept salvation—even though I did not quite know as yet what salvation was—if God would give me overnight success in my sales efforts.

Bud and I continued to attend church together, both morning and evening as well as the youth society meetings. That following Sunday, at the evening meeting, I seemed to hear Mrs. Long's words in the songs, the prayers, the sermon. The church was what you might call old line, giving emphasis on worship Sunday morning, evangelism Sunday night. Evangelism included a call for sinners to come to the altar and make public their renunciation of the old life and acceptance of the new.

Several responded to the Sunday night invitation. I almost joined them.

As we sat parked outside Bud's house, I said, "What happens, Bud? The way some people act when they get . . . saved, like you say . . . it's as if they got hit by an electric shock or something."

"I guess getting saved strikes different people different ways," Bud philosophized. "Like, say at a ball game. One guy yells his tonsils loose while the bird next to him sits like it's a checker game or something. They're both just as interested; they just act different."

"Maybe the silent fellow sees more of the game and gets more out of it than the first," I suggested.

"Could be," Bud agreed.

We sat silently for a few moments.

"So many people have Christianity all confused," I remembered Mrs. Long telling me. "They think it's a lot of do this and don't do that. Stanley, it isn't what you do or don't do that makes you become a Christian. It's what God has done, through Jesus."

One Saturday night, I parked the Model T and Bud and I walked the streets of Lima as we often did.

"Bud," I said, "I've been doing a lot of thinking."

"Yeah? What about?"

"About religion. Christianity, I mean, the way they preach it at that church you go to."

Bud was quiet.

"You ever think about it," I inquired, "as something for yourself, I mean?"

"Uh, well," Bud hesitated, "I got sorta saved myself when I was a kid in grade school."

"Aren't you saved now?" I asked.

"I guess I am."

We came walking past an ice cream store.

"Buy you a malt?" I asked.

Bud nodded.

We entered. We got our malts—the thick kind you can only eat with a spoon—then sat quietly for several minutes.

"You know somethin', Bud?" I began.

"No, what?" he asked.

"Tomorrow night in church," I blurted, "I'm going to get this salvation business settled."

"You are?" Bud looked at me in a kind of wonderment.

"I need you to help me, though."

"How can I do that?"

"I want us to sit together, like we always do, and I want to sit next to the aisle. When the preacher gives the altar call for sinners to come forward, I want you to give me a good shove."

"You want me to do what?" Bud questioned.

"Give me a good shove out into the aisle," I said. "If you give me that, I think I can make it the rest of the way."

I took a long walk alone that following Sunday afternoon. Time passed quickly. The hour neared for the evening service. Conflicting emotions disturbed my mind. There were times I anticipated the service and times I became apprehensive. But of one thing I was sure: I would attend and I would respond to the salvation call.

But let me get back to the events of that significant evening. The two of us arrived just as the song leader announced the first hymn. We sat near the back, I on the aisle as planned, my cousin directly beside me.

I'd be at a loss to tell you what the preacher talked about that night. It hardly seemed as though we were in a church meeting. It was more like some kind of suspended animation. So during the whole sermon, I had the feeling the preacher singled me out the way a hunter does when he aims at a flock of geese.

It was miserable, yet reassuring, for God was bringing into fruition the simple prayer of that boy who, driving the milk cows home from the pasture one night, looked at the rising glow of the moon and whispered, "Where are You, God? I sure would like to know You."

God is God. What a revitalizing thought! He loves us and wants us to come to know Him and to love Him. He may lead over variant circumstances but He will meet any person who sincerely seeks to find Him.

He met me that night.

When the invitation was given, I didn't wait for Bud's nudge. I bolted out from the pew and down the aisle. Stanley Tam had never been more serious in his whole life!

A counselor met me. We knelt. He reviewed some of the same Bible verses Mrs. Long had introduced to me.

"Talk to the Lord," he said tenderly, "just as you talk to me. Tell him what you understand and what you want."

"Lord," I prayed, "I'm a sinner. I know I can't earn my salvation. That's why you sent Jesus into the world. I accept Jesus as my personal Savior."

I lifted my head and slowly opened my eyes. I was a bit confused.

The counselor turned the pages of his Bible to the book of Romans as Mrs. Long had done, asking me, "What does it say here?"

"Whosoever shall call upon the name of the Lord," I began.

"Did you call on the name of the Lord?" he asked.

"I sure did."

"Then what's happened to you?"

"I . . ."

"You called, right?"

"I did."

"You meant what you said in your prayer?"

"Sure did."

"Do you believe the Lord heard you?"

"Sure hope so."

"It's more than hoping so, Stanley. God plainly tells you that if you call, He will answer. So if from a sincere heart you called upon the Lord, what happened to you?"

The truth of what had taken place began to get through to me. I felt a spontaneous smile come to my face.

"What happened, Stanley?" the counselor prodded gently.

"I became a Christian," I replied. A shiver of delight throbbed through my chest. Tears came to my eyes.

Stanley Tam was born again!

C H A P T E R

E I G H T

Afterglow

In my own case, I had the wonderful experience of becoming a know-so Christian from the time I knelt at that church altar in the early autumn of 1933 until this very moment. The Bible tells us in Romans 8:16 the Spirit Himself "testifies with our spirit that we are God's children."

Actually, it is good to have honest doubts. In First Thessalonians 5:21, we are invited to "prove all things; hold fast that which is good" (KJV). The conversion experience involves an enormous leap from the finite to the infinite, during which time a convert remains essentially the same person as before. If you had problems with patience, you will continue to have moments of impatience. If you had a quick temper, you are not likely to overcome it instantly.

There is one tremendous difference. Through the presence of the Holy Spirit, Christ begins a process of change. "Therefore if any man be in Christ," the Bible assures us in Second Corinthians 5:17, "he is a new creature: old things are passed away; behold, all things are become new" (KJV).

I didn't have a lot of "old things" needing to pass out of my life. I didn't smoke, didn't drink. I was morally clean, honest, trustworthy. I was what you would call a righteous young man.

Ah, but never forget what the Bible says about human righteousness. Isaiah 64:6 tells us, "We are all as an unclean thing, and all our righteousnesses are as filthy rags" (KJV). The point is one which Mrs. Long made very clear to me: We can only become Christians and qualify for heaven by receiving forgiveness for our sinful natures, however noble our good works may be.

You see, Jesus died on the cross so we could change from being earthly people to heavenly people. In short, from sinners to Christians.

Shortly after my conversion, I found that Bible verse in Second Peter 3:18 which says, "Grow in grace, and in the knowledge of our Lord and Saviour Jesus Christ" (KJV). Here's how it works.

We have a foundation. We build upon that foundation, as the Bible states it so clearly:

> For other foundation can no man lay than that is laid, which is Jesus Christ. Now if any man build upon this foundation gold, silver, precious stones, wood, hay, stubble; every man's work shall be made manifest: for the day shall declare it, because it shall be revealed by fire; and the fire shall try every man's work of what sort it is. (1 Corinthians 3:11-13, KJV)

Building upon the correct foundation not only validates our Christian lives but nurtures us as well, so that we experience vital and vigorous growth.

My Christian faith never became what you would call an emotional experience. My preference is to look at a proposition squarely, analyze it, put it to the test, believe what I see to be true and reject what I find to be untrue. As I've gone through life I've noticed that a lot of folks suffer religious maladjustment because they somehow get the idea that faith is a synonym for conformity, not realizing that faith in Christ makes us eligible for the most rewarding of all human fellowship.

But when He relates us to each other in fellowship, God never uses a cookie cutter. Every Christian is meant to be a bona fide original. We may become models for others to follow but never blueprints. God does not make any two Christians exactly alike.

Don't miss the point of what it means to "Grow in grace, and in the knowledge of our Lord and Saviour Jesus Christ" (2 Peter 3:18, KJV). Growth means submitting to His plan for our lives—His design, His workmanship, not ours.

In my early days as a growing Christian, I did have questions. I don't know that you can call them doubts, because I was so sure of my relationship to the Lord. I've long remembered the words of the counselor who helped me come to the point of decision at that church altar.

"Assurance must be in God's Word," he said, "not in hopes or feelings."

The whole purpose of the Bible is to state God's conditions and provisions, not only for the beginning of the life in Christ but also for the continuity of this life. So, frankly, as I've indicated, various aspects of my Christian experience involved uncertainty and frustration, but as I began studying the Bible, those doubts dissipated and a solidity of faith took their place.

But only the Bible can lead us to such an assurance and bring us through a progressive spiritual maturity.

I became involved in church activities and never missed services. Many times a good sermon stimulated me to a higher spiritual resolve. I'm old-fashioned enough, by the way, to believe adults should attend Sunday school. When a Christian learns how to get alone with the Bible, to dig into it and seek inexhaustible treasures of inspiration and counsel, he cannot help but experience spiritual maturity.

Now, of course, I'm aware of the maelstrom of arguments thrown at the Bible these days. Is it *the* Word of God, or does it only contain the Word of God? Has it become at best an historical record of man's relentless search for meaning about himself and his purpose in the world? Frankly, I have neither the time nor the scholarly background to participate in such discussions. If the Bible is the living Word of God, it is equal to whatever test of accuracy men may feel inclined to give it. Keep in mind, however, that, in the final analysis, it is not the test so called scholars give to the Bible that counts, but the spirituality of those people which prompts giving the test in the first place.

"Keep thy heart with all diligence," the Bible cautions us, "for out of it are the issues of life" (Proverbs 4:23, KJV). The Bible tells us in Romans 10:17 that "faith comes from hearing the message, and the message is heard through the word of Christ." I am convinced that much of the confusion about the validity of the Bible would evaporate if people would simply come to God's Word, realizing their need for light, recognizing that the Bible is the light they need and let God cleanse and motivate them through His Word.

I sometimes suspect God purposely made it difficult for the natural mind to accept the Bible as His inspired Book. Crossing the Red Sea, the big fish experience of Jonah, the miracles of the New Testament—all have a disciplinary effect upon the quest for faith by compelling us to come to God in humility, recognizing that God is God and nothing is too difficult for Him.

Let's leave the theological disputes to others.

Join me, if you will, in a method of Bible exploration which has energized my spiritual life during these many years of walking with the Lord. For me, the key to unlocking the in-depth teachings and meanings of the Bible lies in the exploration of the wonderful experience called meditation. I often spend an hour on one verse of the Bible, possibly even on a phrase or just one word. I ask God to make the meaning clear to me—not the theological meaning or the doctrinal meaning, but the relevance to my own life and to God's plan for my life.

What does the Scripture say to me in the matter of guidance? Does it point out a weakness in my personality needing to be corrected? Or is it a window, framing the greatness of the Lord in a display I may not have seen before?

Through meditation the Bible becomes imminently relevant. God's Word not only provides firm ground on which to plant my faith, but, as I discovered in those early efforts in meditation, I began to sense heartening changes in my life.

My innately negative attitude began to take a positive trend. I became more outgoing, more poised, more aware of the purpose of life.

I'm sure it is true of most Christians that, during those early months following conversion, one makes many discoveries of the promises God gives in His Word.

I remember finding one such promise in the twelfth chapter of Romans, after struggling through the thought-provoking issues in that marvelous book. I also discovered the many gems contained in the shorter epistles of the New Testament, such as Philippians 4:19, "My God shall supply all your need according to his riches in glory by Christ Jesus" (KJV).

What a transforming moment it was the time I first read Galatians 5:22-23: "The fruit of the spirit is love, joy, peace, patience, kindness, goodness, faithfulness, gentleness and self-control."

Early in my Christian life, I got into the Old Testament. It has so many difficult things to understand, that major section of God's Word, and I admit I struggled many times. Of course, I had a great experience with Psalms and Proverbs. Also the majestic book of Isaiah.

I especially remember Jeremiah 29:11—" 'I know the thoughts that I think toward you,' says the LORD, 'thoughts of peace and not of evil, to give you a future and a hope' " (NKJV).

I learned early in my Christian life that friends and advisors can be helpful but can also ill-advise and thus hinder the Holy Spirit's work in my life. For example, shortly after my conversion, the pastor came to me and said, "I've been praying much about you, Stanley, and have a strong conviction in my heart that you should prepare for the ministry. You are just the right age."

Prepare for the ministry? To be a preacher?

I do not recall ever rejecting the idea. On the other hand I had no sense of God calling me. Our pastor made a big thing over the "fact" of God calling Stanley Tam into the ministry. He included it in his pulpit prayers, brought it up at mid-week, talked about it in conversations with members.

He checked me out on such Scriptures as Acts 18:9 where the Lord guided the Apostle Paul through a vision. There was a Bible college in Fort Wayne, which is now a campus for Taylor University, and the pastor suggested that I look into that as a possibility for preparation.

I told him I would do it. But shortly before going over to Fort Wayne, a couple of things happened. First, a couple from our church stopped me on the street and bluntly asked, "Stanley, are you sure God is calling you into the ministry?"

"Well, I don't know," I replied, "I'm such a new Christian. The pastor says I should. Some of the people in the church do too. I feel I'd better check out the Bible school in Fort Wayne."

Then they asked a question that stumped me. "If you are not completely sure that God is calling you into the ministry, how can you trust Him for the money to go to Bible school?" I couldn't answer them.

I decided to go to Fort Wayne and check out the Bible school itself, and ask the people at the college what they advised.

The highway from Lima to Fort Wayne passed through the little town of Delphos. Instantly, my conscience wrenched as I remembered something.

The fifty-five members of my high school graduating class had taken a bus to Delphos for their graduation pictures at a small photography studio which had given us a better price quote than any photographer in our town.

As the bus pulled up to the photography studio, Barney—Mr. Big in our class—threw out a challenge to several of us guys. "Hey, you birds," he said, "I challenge you to steal something from one of these rinky stores before we go back to Lima, somethin' little, just for kicks."

That left me out: Apart from a cookie or two out of my mother's kitchen when I was a kid, I'd never stolen anything in my whole life. "You too, Tam!" Barney snarled. "Don't you go givin' me that holy look!"

I winked at Barney, giving him an OK sign with my left hand.

We had plenty of time waiting for everyone to have the pictures taken, determined not to be laughed at, I sauntered out onto the street and shuffled my way past a couple of stores, coming to a men's shop which looked promising.

"Something I can help you with?" a clerk asked.

"Just lookin' for now," I said.

"You live here in Delphos?"

"No," I replied. "I'm from Lima. Our graduating class is having their pictures taken."

"That's nice," the man smiled broadly. "Thanks for choosing our town." He turned and walked away. In that moment I took a scarf, on sale for a dollar, and stuffed it into my pocket.

The memory of those moments came back to me like the come-to-order at the sound of a judge's gavel. I knew I had to stop and make restitution.

I found the same clothing store and the same clerk. He listened wide-eyed as I told him what I had done, what had happened to me and paid him the amount owed. With abounding joy in my heart, I drove on to Fort Wayne.

After I checked in at the desk, I was immediately taken to the dean's office. "Mr. Tam?" he greeted. "I'm Mr. Lightner. Please sit down."

I told him my whole story. He asked numerous questions. We were together for two hours. I concluded, saying, "I'm willing to do whatever the Lord wants me to, but I sure don't think I could ever be a preacher. I couldn't say ten words in front of an audience."

Mr. Lightner took my hand, gripped it firmly as he said, "Son, I agree with you. The Lord is not calling you into the ministry, and I suggest you not go to Bible school."

A soothing, energizing peace filled my heart. I sensed anew God's call for me to major in business. Indeed, my Lord was guiding me into the school of faith, where he had much to teach me.

NINE

Entering a New World

Obviously disappointed over the decision I had made in Fort Wayne, the pastor assigned me to a young couple for discipling. Although engaged to be married, they had a strictly Victorian romance. They didn't so much as touch hands in public. Discipleship, for them, consisted mainly of telling me about all of the things you shouldn't do as a Christian: no movies, no dances, no card playing, no Sunday swimming—all these things were taboo. Needless to say, that well-meaning couple changed my social life.

In my sincerity to become a genuinely committed Christian, I was willing to give up anything. It was just that I saw abundant Christian living as something positive rather than negative.

Actually, my parents, both of them nonbelievers, rigidly observed Sunday as the Lord's Day. My father wouldn't think of doing any field work, not even when he fell behind in seasonal tilling. Sometimes, for example, the hay would be cut and dried and ready to load and bring into the barn, with perhaps a load or two brought in Saturday afternoon but much remaining to be gathered. Sunday would be a beautiful day, with rain forecast for Monday and, sure enough, come Monday, rain would fall and soak the harvest which should have been gathered on Sunday. This was particularly the case with corn cultivating, when rain would delay work in the fields. Many surrounding farmers got up early Sunday morning and went out to cultivate, knowing that very likely Monday and Tuesday would bring drenching rain once more, but not my father.

I certainly do not consider myself a legalist. There is nothing anyone can do to merit personal salvation. Ephesians 2:8-9 lovingly rebukes anyone who thinks otherwise, with the awesome declaration that "by grace are ye saved through faith, and that not of yourselves; it is the gift of God, not of works, lest anyone should boast" (KJV). From the onset of our marriage, both my wife and I have fully agree with James 4:4: "friendship with the world is enmity with God" (NKJV). Neither of us has attended a public theater since our conversion. We believe Sunday should be observed as the Lord's Day and not as a day of pleasure for yourself.

I know this is old-fashioned so I don't criticize that couple assigned by the pastor to look after my spiritual development. They were the couple that had questioned my planning to go to Bible school. I deeply appreciated their discernment about any calling to the ministry.

My struggle for spiritual development confused my cousin Bud. Were it not for my being so gung-ho on cars, he might have given me a complete write-off sooner than he did. Instead, he stuck with me as we finished work on my initial Model T, giving it a complete tune-up, a stem to stern paint job, plus adding a bit of gingerbread here and there.

Then I found another Model T for sale, slightly beat-up but needing the type of "tender loving care" Bud and I could give it. The owner, however, was so hard pressed for cash he wouldn't sell it on consignment. I figured we lost that one until a stylish collegian saw my Ford, made a good bid on it and handed me the cash, so I was able to purchase the second Model T. All in all, I bought, refurbished and sold a half dozen, each for a profit.

"This is a lot more fun than reclaiming bicycles," I said to Bud.

"Now that you've got religion on your side," Bud replied, "you could make a fortune."

I detected another distinct bite in his voice so did not respond. I didn't always make a profit. A man talked me into letting him take one of my automobiles with only a promise of payment. He never paid a penny, and yet, as Dr. Anderson explained in the first chapter, my eventual mark-up on his transaction totaled more than all the others put together.

We found an elderly lady in the community whose husband had died four years previously. She told the executor of his estate that she didn't want to sell his automobile. So the obliging executor had it pushed into one of the outside buildings. When Bud and I inquired about the automobile, the chickens were gone but they had left their accumulated droppings—a measure for each year— all over the vehicle.

Somehow, we talked the old lady into selling her now filthy automobile, knowing we could clean it up like new. As the lady took several moments to think through the matter, Bud and I looked at each other a moment. I winked at him. He responded with a momentary grin—reminiscent of the old days when we enjoyed such consistent rapport with each other. To our delight and somewhat surprise, the lady accepted our offer and we quickly set to work.

However, I could see how I was slowly but surely losing my cousin's affection. Most of the cars we refurbished we had found pretty much by happenstance. We could not expect to find enough cars to work on a full-time basis. Bud realized too that I could hardly promise to continue the amount I had initially paid him for his services.

Over and above all my costs, I had pocketed a fair amount of profit, and so was giving thought as to what kind of enterprise I should consider. Then came the Sunday afternoon when my sister Evelyn entered the picture. She had a boyfriend who, whenever he called on her, drove his father's car. Of course, the parental automobile wasn't always available. Such was the case one Sunday afternoon when the boyfriend found other means of transportation to get to our place.

"I tell you what let's do, Stanley," my sister said. "Remember that used car lot in town that you showed me, the one that has that beautiful Model T for sale?"

"What about it?" I asked.

Becoming coy as only she could do, my sister continued, "Buy it, Stanley, and loan it once in a while to Browny and me. His job only pays thirty cents an hour, twenty hours a week."

My resistance gave way to pity as, also, my ego flared its haughty head. For I got to thinking: Not only did I love my sister very much, but buying the car and loaning it to her and her boyfriend would be quite a prestigious situation.

"Will you?" Evelyn begged. "It won't hurt to just take a look, will it?"

"Mom will want to know where we've gone," I said. "You know how she is about Sundays."

"I already told her we might go for a walk," Evelyn said.

"The three of us?" I exclaimed. "What kind of a date is that?"

"She seemed to like the idea of you going with us."

"You musn't lie to her," I cautioned.

"I didn't," Evelyn assured.

I glanced into the living room where my father lay asleep on the sofa. Out on the veranda, my mother sat reading a Gene Stratton Porter novel. On Sundays she went to church, did only the most necessary tasks around the house, then rested. Both of them would have staunchly forbidden such profane activity as shopping for an automobile on a Sunday.

My conscience disturbed me just a little. I almost refused, but Evelyn was a subtle little temptress that day, her eyes searching mine with the yearning of a little child pleading to its parent. I couldn't resist her. And so, slipping out the back door, we headed on foot to the used car lot three miles away.

Sitting out on prominent display was the Model T we had previously seen. I thought Evelyn's eyes were going to pop out of her head!

I felt like Henry Ford himself as I laid down the cash for full payment. The transaction was very simple and, in minutes, we drove away—boyfriend Browny sitting at the wheel as though he owned the car.

"You got money for gas?" I asked Browny.

He lurched back, having probably not thought about fuel until that moment. "I've got enough for a couple of gallons," he responded.

I can't ever remember a tank being full on any of my cars.

When my sister and her boyfriend borrowed the car, they used their own gas can. Browny would measure the amount in the tank, mark the point on a stick, then pour in their own gas. When the two came back from a date, they would drain out their gas to the previous mark on the stick. It never occurred to them to pay for wear and tear on the vehicle.

I frequently visited Mrs. Long, who proved to be an adept counselor. So wise she was, so practical. She didn't contradict the counsel of the married couple from church, but in her winsome manner, infused a more positive influence into my young and struggling faith.

Even though I was such a neophyte Christian, I had a yearning in my heart to win souls. I would lie in bed at night and imagine myself going door to door with a Bible rather than my sample case, but I also imagined myself going through life, like so many Christians, without bringing anyone to the Savior.

If I ever did venture out and try to win someone to Christ, I determined Mrs. Long would be my model.

One day when I stopped at her home for a chat, she told me why she had witnessed to me when I came to her home on that first occasion. "There had come a time in my life," she said, "when I wanted to be a soul winner more than anything I could think of. But everything seemed to be against me. My husband was a hired hand on this farm and he only made $8 a week, there was no extra money to buy gasoline to drive to town to do personal evangelism. The houses are too far apart out here in the country to go door to door. Also I had nobody to take care of my two little children. But the desire burned in my heart and I thought *I have to be a soul winner.*

"One day, I went into my bedroom. I made an altar to God. I got down on my knees and prayed, 'God, I have to be a soul winner, but everything is against me. No money for gasoline to go to town, houses out here are too far apart to go door to door, then there is nobody to take care of my two little children. So here is what I am going to do. On this altar, I am placing my front room. I am asking you to bring lost souls to my door.' Stanley, you are the seventh one that the Holy Spirit has brought to my front door that has accepted Christ as his personal Savior."

That's pretty serious business, don't you think? All our houses have doors. People come to those doors. Many of them are lost, possibly even seeking for special peace.

That lovely woman's sincerity tore at my heart, becoming the predominant inspiration for the career God would one day give me in outreach evangelism.

"What are we doing about it?" Mrs. Long asked me that day. Her question would linger long in my thoughts, hounding me, demanding a reply I was unable to give. Let me hasten to add, however, Mrs. Long became by no means a negative force in my life. She could inspire a person by remaining completely positive in her counsel.

Meanwhile, I added a new dimension to my farm earnings. Whether or not I sold any of my products, I would ask if there might be old metal, dead batteries and other items of junk I could buy. This always made a hit, because farmers didn't seem to know how simple it was to take such items to a junk dealer and turn them into cash. Sometimes, when I paid a farmer for the junk he was selling me, he would use the money to purchase some of my products which he had previously refused.

I would take note of mailboxes when I entered a place, and if I found one in unusually bad condition would offer to paint the farmer's name on the box. Farmers like to see their names identified with their farms. I played that fact to its ultimate, asking a farmer if he would like to see his name painted in eight-foot letters on the side of the barn. This made a real hit, plus created a nice increase in my cash earnings.

The expanding dimension of my success with farmers lifted my spirits considerably. Yet, deep inside, I had a dream. I didn't want to go around begging people for their business. I wanted to be an entrepreneur of some sort with people coming to me instead of my going to them.

One day I came home to be met by my father holding a book. "I bought this for you, Stanley," he said, handing me the volume. I looked at the cover. *One Thousand Products You Can Manufacture*.

"It looks interesting to me," he said, "and I thought it might light a fire in your fertile brain." Such an expression of love and caring from my father set my heart aglow.

I found the book fascinating, as my father had predicted. It gave procedures for manufacturing such things as shoe polish, glue and penetrating oil. Oil caught my fancy, mostly because it involved taking a worthless product, namely waste oil, and transforming it into a profitable entity. Following carefully the instructions in the book, I went to a filling station and asked for old oil from oil changes which they were glad to provide at no charge, rather than go through the details of properly disposing elsewhere.

All I had to do was filter the waste oil through an old felt hat. It was a slow process. I estimated it could take a week for one gallon to filter through, so I got a lot of old hats to filter the oil. My estimation was not far off!

Once I reached the middle stage of production, I added muriatic acid and just like that, many gallons of penetrating oil resulted.

I sold the handsome-looking product to merchants by the quart, calling my company Tam-O-Shanter Oil Company. I worked hard, producing large quantities of the penetrating oil.

Initial sales were good, but then reality struck. A quart of penetrating oil could last a merchant five to ten years, making resale to the same customers nearly impossible. So the Tam-O-Shanter Oil Company went the way of all of my off-the-cuff schemes. But Tam-O-Shanter would one day be revived.

Meanwhile, I began another company which I called the Micro Slide Company. In the early days of this past century, photographers took portrait

51

photos on glass plates, which were covered with a sensitive emulsion. These plates were made in Belgium, on the best glass in the world. There could be no blemishes of any kind in the glass or the photographic image would be marred. After a photographer exposed a portrait on one of the glass plates, he kept it on file for as much as ten years. After that, they were discarded as junk.

I, however, got the idea of buying them. I dipped the discarded plates in a special chemical solution which removed the emulsion and left the glass exactly the proper thickness for micro slides. I made a jig to cut them to the right size.

A problem arose, however, when I realized the disparity between what it cost me to manufacture a thousand plates and the price I might expect to obtain from selling them. In other words, I had duped myself into a manufacturing scheme which looked good enough at the outset, but gave no promise of ever making enough profit to merit continuing.

I was back once again to square one. Worse than that, however, I began to suspect that Stanley Tam didn't have it, and anything I tried would be doomed to failure.

CHAPTER

TEN

Looking for a Job

I was converted at the Christian and Missionary Alliance Church in Lima because that was where Bud attended and where he invited and brought me. It was strange and distressing that Bud played such a prominent role in my conversion and yet, at the same time, his own spiritual life was going into decline. In retrospect I realize that, had I not been such a fledgling believer myself, I surely would have tried to help him. The stage was set for us to enjoy a lifetime fellowship. Bud might well have found a spot in our organization. We could have traveled together, ministered together, building upon the foundation established in our childhood. But, unfortunately, as I grew in the Christian life, Bud drifted away until he seemed to abandon his faith completely. Not until he was in his sixties did he come back to the Lord.

My enthusiasm for anything involving Christianity grew rapidly. I thrived on church activities, had near perfect attendance at Sunday school, relished Sunday morning worship services and evening evangelism and faithfully attended the midweek prayer and Bible study. Shyness continued to hinder me, however. Nothing made me more reticent than to be in the presence of robust Christians who, in Sunday school or at midweek, spoke openly about their thoughts as believers in Christ. I managed an occasional word of witness, sometimes gave an audible prayer, but mostly participated in silence.

Although I struggled with farm-to-farm and even some door-to-door attempts at selling, I had decided I must find a place of employment where I could put in my hours and receive an assured weekly check. I never missed mid-week in the hope that such faithfulness to that night on the church's weekly schedule would somehow qualify me for an answer to my private prayers. I remember how on many Wednesday nights when the pastor would ask if anyone had a special request, I had tried to raise my hand but couldn't.

Finally, one Wednesday night, I could refrain no longer.

"Remember when I have told you many times," the pastor said, "when we refuse to make our prayer request known to our brothers and sisters in Christ, we may be denying them great blessings. It is a joy to pray for one another, a blessing to see how God answers our prayers."

Up went my hand.

"What is it, Stanley?" he asked.

My tongue went thick in my mouth.

"Let us help you," he continued. "God answers prayer."

"Amen!" someone piped up.

All eyes turned to me. I'm sure they looked in sympathy but I sat as a prisoner at the dock. Finally, I managed to blurt, "I need a job." So the people spent several moments praying for me. Their prayers were beautiful and full of faith.

We had a middle-aged spinster in our church. She had remained unclaimed for numerous and obvious reasons. As soon as the pastor dismissed the midweek meeting that night, she came bolting toward me at a zealous momentum to ask, "Do you fast and pray, Stanley?"

"Uh . . . I . . ." I tried to answer. I had heard of fasting through Sunday school lessons but had never given the matter any serious thought.

"Well," she primed, "do you?" I could only stare at her, whereupon she devoted several minutes to a summary of those times, particularly in the New Testament, when the followers of Jesus had reinforced their prayers with fasting. "I could never possibly be the Christian I am today," she intoned, "if it wasn't for my fasting and praying."

I wanted to break away but the woman held me as though in a spell.

"Land sakes," she half-scorned, "how do you ever hope to grow in your Christian life, much less get your prayers answered, if you don't practice fasting and prayer?" I continued standing there, speechless.

"Do you know what fasting is?"

"Not really, ma'am." She turned as if to summon the pastor, then apparently decided to go it alone. "Fasting means just what it says," she continued, not realizing how confusing such a statement was to a young believer. "You go without food and you spend the time praying. I do it all the time." She went into an elongated explanation of her fasting procedure. Vague though her discourse was, I began to get the gist of the subject. I remembered Elijah in the wilderness, and Jesus, fasting before He was tempted by the devil.

"How do I do it?" I asked.

"You don't eat," was the blunt reply. "When everybody else goes to the table, you go away someplace and pray. You don't talk about it. Do you hear me, Stanley? If somebody asks you why you aren't eating, you don't dare say it's because you're fasting. Fasting is a secret between you and your heavenly Father. There is no more sure way of breaking the power of fasting and prayer than to brag about it to other people. That's what the Pharisees did, they made it as public as they could so people would see them as being especially righteous."

I turned to leave but she snatched my shirt sleeve and held me another moment. "You do it, Stanley, now that you've got the Lord's light on the subject. You do it. Do it tomorrow."

"Yes, ma'am," I half-whispered, then turned and made a sprightly exit from the church.

I awakened the next morning with an abounding appetite. From downstairs wafted the aroma of pancakes. I knew my mother had had me in mind when she made them. Often she made them just because she knew how much I liked those mixed from a recipe she kept in her heart. My mouth watering, I began putting on my clothes. Then, as I leaned to pick up a pair of socks, I saw myself in the dresser mirror and stopped dead as I remembered the fasting pledge.

So I solemnly finished dressing, then headed out of my room toward the stairway. What would I do? Pretend illness? I knew I couldn't resort to falseness in any way.

When I reached the bottom of the stairs, I could see she had gone to the pantry. I should have dashed headlong toward the door but instead I stood, confused, as my mother returned to the kitchen.

"I figured the smell of your favorite breakfast would rouse you out," she said happily.

"I'm not having any breakfast," I told her.

She looked at me in a mix of curiosity and disbelief, as she asked, "You sick?"

"Nope." She came up to me and felt my forehead, reached for my pulse. "I'm not sick," I said.

She pulled my chair from the table and tried to pull me into it. "Sit up to the table, Stanley. Those on top are pipin' hot."

"I'm not hungry, Ma," I told her. My conscience twitched. Christian or no Christian, honesty came as naturally to me as breath.

She came to me, placed her hand on my forehead a second time, and then said, "Not a smidgen of fever."

I hurried away, reached the back door where I turned toward the kitchen and called out, "I won't be home for lunch or supper!"

My mother stood at the back door hands on hips, watching in astounded displeasure as I drove out of the yard. I headed out into the country, familiar territory I had traversed many times. I drove miserably at first, as the pangs of appetite tormented my stomach with anguished hunger. Thinking it might help to drive faster, I pressed the foot feed. It didn't help and I slowed down again.

I pulled off to the side of the road and turned off the ignition. Farmers came driving by, slowing down to look at me and see if I might be in need. One farmer stopped. "Motor broke down?" he asked.

"Motor's fine," I replied.

"Then why are you just sitting here?"

"Thinking," I replied. He looked at me a long moment, as though there was some kind of stigma to parking alongside a country road to sit quietly and think. I thought to start the car and drive away, but he drove away first and so I stayed.

At last, I drove back into town, parked on the main street and browsed in a few stores. In my strolling along the street itself, I came past what we called a greasy spoon restaurant. In no way could it be considered gourmet or appealing. That afternoon, however, the aroma of frying food wafted out the door and directly into my nostrils. In years to come, not the finest cuisine would be more appealing.

I hesitated a moment, debating whether or not to enter. Lest I yield to temptation, I hurried to my car. I thought of driving home and going to my room where I could get an afternoon nap. Mostly I never slept in the daytime, except those days when long, drenching rains lingered hour upon hour. On such days, I would sleep as though I had taken a sleeping pill.

Despite the fact that we were not estranged, I rarely drove to my cousin Bud's house anymore. That day, wanting to get away from the temptation of food, I drove directly to his place. Wouldn't you know? They were having early supper!

"Hey," Bud called out pleasantly, "pull up another chair."

"We've got plenty," Aunt Blanche added.

"No thanks," I replied. I sauntered into the living room.

"Something you had for lunch upset your stomach?" Bud called.

"I didn't have any lunch," I said before I could censor myself.

"He's sick for sure," I heard Bud say to his parents.

"I'll be OK," I assured my relatives. Then I dropped into a Lazy Boy, picked up the day's newspaper and turned to the comics. The Popeye cartoon was called Thimble Theater in those days. It featured Popeye and his girlfriend Olive Oyl. Popeye was always refurbishing his amazing strength with cans of spinach. His friend Wimpy, on the other hand, thrived on hamburgers and was frequently heard to say, "I would gladly pay you Tuesday for a hamburger today." The thought of the hamburger tantalized my gastric juices.

So I disciplined my attention to other comics. "You can at least eat some of this," I heard him saying, and looked up to see him holding out a bowl of tapioca pudding, which he deftly shoved into my hands before hurrying back to the dinner table. In that moment I forgot about fasting and was about to consume the delicacy, but I caught myself just in time.

Quickly, I tore an advertising page out of the paper and, carefully dumping the contents of the bowl onto it and folding the paper put it into my pocket for later disposal. Then I took the bowl back to the kitchen.

"Boy, you ate that fast," Bud said.

"You must have been hungry." Aunt Blanche added, "We can give you some seconds."

"No thanks," I responded, and then I excused myself. I went outside to my car, and proceeded home at a leisurely pace. When I entered the house, I found my parents in the front room.

"Is that you, Stanley?" my mother called out. When I identified myself, she added, "Have you had food?"

"I'm OK," I replied and went up the stairs.

The hunger kept me awake seemingly for hours, and gave me a headache. But eventually I slept. It troubled me to realize that, so taken with hunger, I had devoted very little time to prayer. Were not prayer and fasting to be in juxtaposition?

Mercifully, the next morning I again awakened to the aroma of pancakes. I jumped out of bed and must have set a new record getting dressed and down the stairs. I remember people in the Bible fasting for many days, but the lady at church had mentioned only one day, so I devoured two platefuls of pancakes while my faith dwindled as to the likelihood of a job resulting from my prior day's hunger ordeal.

It was Saturday. That night, as was always my custom, I drove downtown and joined a couple of friends to walk the streets. Back and forth we walked, up and down. Then, an amazing thing happened. A stranger came up behind us and tapped me on the shoulder. I stepped back to join him. My friends broke stride a moment, glancing back at me in curiosity, then moved on.

"You looking for work, son?" the stranger asked.

"I sure am!" I told him.

"We have a job for you down at White Mountain Dairy, testing cream. You'll get on to how it's done real easy and there's nothing to it. If you're interested, be there first thing Monday."

Thinking back, I have questions. Did that one day of fasting really result in my strange encounter with the man on the street? Or was it happenstance? All I know is that I was set free from the drudgery of going door-to-door and farm-to-farm trying to sell items that few people had any desire to buy.

It was an instructive time in my life. For though I was spared the drudgery of selling, I realized I was making considerably less money than I did representing kitchen products and kindred items. Then too my job became boring. The thought came to mind that I should go back to calling on farmers again.

Would I ever find peace in my heart? Did people who truly discovered the will of God for their lives become free of emptiness and anxiety? The couple charged with discipling me tried to counsel me in such matters. One night following the Sunday evening service, the lady caught my eye and indicated she wished to talk to me. "Have you heard about Montgomery Ward having job openings?" she said. "Why don't you check?"

I did the next morning and was hired on the spot. They placed me up in the automotive department, changing tires, batteries and oil. It seemed ideal. I was working in the specific areas of my top expertise, forty hours a week for twenty eight cents an hour.

I did well, was about on the verge of advancement, when I had a bit of a problem. One day when I was working on the goods receiving dock, I checked in a shipment of living room suites. The truck driver told me there were three complete suites. I took his word and signed the freight bill without counting the pieces. When the manager discovered that only two complete suites had been delivered, he fired me.

Lessons to Learn

I have come to see the Christian life as three-dimensional: first, reading the Bible; next, giving quality time for prayer; finally, witnessing to lost souls about my faith in Christ.

Oh, I did pray. A lot.

And my prayers primarily involved my insatiable desire to become successful and affluent. When the offering plate passed through my pew on Sunday morning, I put in my mite's worth, often praying silently, "But Lord, just think if You would give me $10,000 a year, I would have $1,000 to give to Your work."

I have long since learned that the most effective prayers do not involve self-interest. In First Corinthians 10:31, the Bible tells us, "Whether therefore ye eat, or drink, or whatsoever ye do, do all to the glory of God" (KJV) In no aspect of life does that admonition relate more forcefully than in the things about which we pray.

"To the glory of God." If I made selfish requests to the Lord, how could I be praying for His glory? How could I glorify Him by complaining in my prayers?

As time passed, I did experience some faltering growth. I studied Sunday school lessons more arduously than I had ever done lessons at school. I listened intently to the sermons at church, gave full attention to midweek Bible studies. Yet I remained bewildered, unable to put things together. I thought of consulting the pastor but didn't have the courage to approach him.

Worst of all, as I have told you, my cousin Bud moved progressively out of my life. Even now I think back to the kind of fellowship we might have had.

The Lord was putting me through a crucible of experiences, validating such Scriptures as First Thessalonians 5:18, "In every thing give thanks: for this is the will of God in Christ Jesus concerning you" (KJV).

For example, just prior to my dismissal from Montgomery Ward, I left work engrossed in wishful thinking. Foolishly, I jaywalked across the street without paying any attention to traffic. A passing automobile hit me broadside, knocking me down. My elbow broke one of the headlights on the automobile. The driver came rushing back to check on me.

"Are you badly hurt?" he wanted to know.

I lay stunned for several moments as a crowd began surrounding me from all sides. As I slowly gathered my senses, I looked up at the crowd staring down at me like patrons at a county fair freak show. Suddenly I caught enough of my wits to stumble to my feet and run toward my car a block away. I heard the screech of another motor, as a second driver succeeded in avoiding hitting me.

Although in considerable pain, I managed the seven blocks to my home.

"What's wrong?" my mother exclaimed the moment I crept inside the house.

"I was hit," I told her.

"Hit?"

"By a car."

I scurried and stumbled to my bed, my mother trailing after me. It was getting to be a time when physicians didn't come to you, but you came to them. Quite unable at the moment to get me to a doctor or hospital, my mother made as thorough an examination as she knew how to do and, finally determining that I had no broken bones, made me comfortable before going downstairs to fix a cup of hot broth. I remained in bed several days.

Recapping the accident in my mind, I realized I could have broken my legs or my back or could even have knocked my head on the pavement severely enough to kill me.

A lull came into my Christian life and as time went on my spiritual enthusiasm waned. I needed a counselor, someone who would stand by me and guide me. Since my time as a young Christian, churches have improved in the follow-up of new converts. In my time, however, it seemed we were to make it on our own, to be faithful in attendance in church and to pay attention to information given in services and Sunday school with no one to help us integrate the teaching into our lives.

I met some young fellows my age who attended another church in Lima and claimed to be Christians. However, they had not rid their lives of a penchant for outright devilment. They lived at the very edge of town, and behind their house the streetcar ended its run. The motorman conductor didn't need to turn the car around however, but simply took his cashbox to the opposite end of the conveyance and retraced the route over which he had just come. There were controls at both ends of the car.

He sometimes waited ten minutes or so before beginning the route back, depending upon the time of day and the frequency of streetcar travel during that period. That is where my friends and I entered the scene.

"We have some great fun, Stanley," the leader of the group told me, "and don't hurt anybody or anything."

The streetcar got its electrical power from heavy electric trolley wires overhead, and my friends told me it was a simple matter to pull down the trolley bar and plunge the trolley into darkness, plus shutting off the power supply to the electric motors.

Tingling with excitement, I followed my new friends through the darkness to a point about ten yards from the dormant trolley. As the conductor stepped to the front of his car and prepared to retrace his route back into town, we pulled the bar off of the trolley wire. Considerable electric current ran through those wires, and pulling the bar off the wire caused a streak like lightning to light up the area.

We hid in weeds nearby, watching as the conductor stumbled out into the darkness and to the rear of the trolley. He fumbled several moments and then found a rope with which he could maneuver the arm overhead and thus maneuver the power bar back onto the electric line.

"We do this all the time," the elder friend whispered. "He gets awful mad but never comes after us." We waited a few moments until the streetcar departed, then walked away from the scene of our devilment.

I'll never know how it happened, but as we emerged from the area, we stepped into the waiting arms of several policemen. To our horror, we were taken to the police station and questioned for over an hour. It seemed almost sacrilegious to be praying about something like the trouble I had gotten myself in, but I seldom prayed harder in my whole life. I can't say my prayer was answered, because I'm not sure, but I do remember being mighty thankful that we were only given a reprimand and then discharged.

I promised God, following that streetcar incident, never again to allow my conduct to become vulnerable to police intervention.

* * *

I was only off work a short time following the Montgomery Ward dismissal when another friend arranged a job for me as an attendant at the largest Sunoco service station in Lima. I liked the job and enjoyed working with my friend.

I worked there for several months and did so well I was eventually named manager. The reason I got the manager's job was because it was the former manager who changed oil on a car and forgot to reinsert the drain nut so when he filled the motor with oil and the owner drove away, all the oil drained out, the motor was ruined and the owner of the station had to purchase a new motor, which cost him so much and irritated him so severely, he fired the manager.

I grew closer to my dad in those days—not what you would call warm rapport, but if he had a sales trip to make on one of my days off, he often asked me to accompany him. He taught me many things about how to survive without money. Indeed, on many of those trips he encountered disappointment, and we would be low or out of cash entirely. He told me, for example, how on one occasion he had traded a tire jack for some gasoline, another when he secured extra cash in exchange for a tire pump.

I remember his coming home from sales trips not having earned so much as a dollar for which to buy groceries, and the look of disdain on my mother's face.

I finally got up enough courage to find myself a girlfriend. She proved my undoing in a different sort of way. I took her one night to a party. I was so excited about it I completely forgot to file my monthly report with the Oil Company Headquarters in Toledo. The next morning I got a telephone call telling me I had been let go.

When times were difficult my father gave me much encouragement. For example, the district manager of the Hoover Vacuum Cleaner Company offered me a job and, as I think back, I realize it would have paid better than anything I had done to that point and also would have been easier and somewhat pleasant.

But my father invariably interrupted at times like this, urging me to keep my options open for the kind of work we both felt I was qualified to do. Strange, when I think of it, the rapport we had with each other, yet we were so distant in other ways.

He encouraged me to stop at photo studios and pick up outdated negatives. I didn't do it full time but as a sideline and it paid me reasonably well. How this worked is that when a photographer assumed the customer would no longer order photographs, he discarded the negative. I picked them up and took them to a firm in Valparaiso, Indiana, where they washed off the gelatin emulsion, leaving the celluloid, which could be cut into squares and sold to billfold manufacturers to be used as identification covers.

As I say, this was only a part-time venture, interspersed with other efforts I extended toward finding some kind of get-rich activity that would set me squarely on the road to success.

One day, as was a common occurrence, I found myself running low on cash. On the positive side, however, I had collected a number of negatives—worth a handsome $80—and decided to take the run to Valparaiso and pick up some change for myself.

I checked the gas and found I had just about enough gas to get to Valparaiso, where I would pick up payment and could buy gas for the trip back home.

I felt quite optimistic as I drove the three hours from home to the Indiana outlet for my materials, and especially remember the lightness of my spirit. I sang hymns, quoted a few of the Bible verses I knew, had a good time thanking the Lord for all His blessings. It was one of my few times of unmitigated optimism. It actually seemed as though everything was moving in my favor for a change.

I reached Valparaiso in the late afternoon, the sun low in the sky for that time of year, and went immediately to the reclamation headquarters, stopping first at the warehouse where I picked up a slip acknowledging my negatives and then jogging to the office.

The girl at the front desk examined my material for a moment and then said, "This is good, Mr. Tam. We'll send you your money first thing Monday."

"Monday?" I half-shouted. "I have to have the money now! I'm broke."

"Oh," the girl responded, "I'm sorry. The boss took his wife into Chicago for the day. They'll be staying over the weekend. He is the only one authorized to write checks." I nearly went into a frenzy.

The phone rang and the girl turned away. I sauntered to a window, looked out at my car, then checked my pocket where I found a dime and three pennies.

I went outside and checked my gas supply. I had about two gallons. No way did I have enough to get me all the way home. Added to that dilemma was the hunger that suddenly came like a fist to my stomach. My plan, of course, had been to use the $80 for a tank full of gas and a man-sized lunch before taking the 180-mile trip back home.

What was I to do? I could leave my car and hitchhike home, but that meant I would need to come back for it. I offered a simple prayer asking, "What should I do, Lord?"

"Drive home, Stanley," I'm sure I heard the Lord tell me. "Trust Me to get you there." There was a hamburger shop nearby which sold hamburgers for a nickel in those days. So I invested five cents toward the increasing hunger in my stomach.

Then I headed into a gas station. The attendant came to my side of the car and, as a good gas salesman should, asked, "Fill 'er up?"

"You, uh," I hesitated, "you wouldn't sell me eight cents worth of gas, would you?"

The attendant looked at me as though making an initial assessment of my sanity. "You won't go very far on eight cents," he cautioned. "Is your tank empty?"

"Not quite," I said, irritated that he should butt into my business.

Reluctantly, he metered out the small amount of fuel into my tank. Then I headed east on Highway 30, lingering a moment at the stop sign as there was no traffic coming up behind me. I bowed my head on the steering wheel. "Lord," I prayed aloud, "I don't have near enough gas to get me back home. But I believe You told me I should go, and I trust You to take care of me."

The prayer lifted my spirits a bit. I resumed driving. It was sundown as I drove out of Valparaiso, dusk coming quickly and then darkness. At a slight variance in the road, my headlights picked up a hitchhiker. Ordinarily I would have pressed the foot feed but, instead, I touched the brake. My father had cautioned—it had almost been a command—never to pick up hitchhikers. I rarely did, but this time I felt a strong sense of direction to do so.

"Hey, fella," the young man exclaimed, as he jumped into my vehicle. "Thanks for stopping. I've been standing here for hours."

I couldn't see him very well in the darkness, but picked out the countenance of someone a bit older than I who seemed a far stretch from being any kind of culprit. "I've been on a short vacation in Chicago. Money is so tight I saved on train fare by hitchhiking. I did OK thumbing my way to Chicago, but coming home has been something else. I started out early this morning, and have been all day getting this far. I live in Marion. How far are you going?"

"Lima," I replied, clearing my throat nervously. "That is, if . . ."

"Why the hesitation?"

So I told him what had happened back in Valparaiso, about not being able to get the money owed me, and about having spent all I had brought along for expenses.

"Look," he said, breaking into a friendly laugh, "I'm no highway bum. Like I told you, I was hitchhiking just to save some expenses. I've got money. Pull into the first gas station we see, and fill 'er up."

God was preparing me for a life of sheer adventure in the wonder of trusting Him to take care of all my needs! That night God taught me the greatest lesson of spiritual success that I have ever been taught. He had his hitchhiker along my pathway to meet all my needs, if I would do one thing, the most important thing: if I would step out in faith and trust God every time that He spoke to my heart. As you read this book, I trust that you will recognize that the scarlet thread running through it is obedience. "To obey is better than sacrifice" (1 Samuel 15:22).

TWELVE

At the Crossroads

Surely I hadn't established a sufficient reputation for anyone to look for me with an employment opportunity. As I reminisce, I'm all the more convinced it had to be the hand of the Good Shepherd, leading me progressively toward the life He had planned for me. Anyway, I was only out of work a short while after being fired by the Sun Oil Company when the district supervisor for the Hoover Company sought me out and offered me a job as one of their salesman.

"How did they ever hear about you?" my father asked.

"Beats me," I replied. "What do you think I should do?"

My father was pensive for a long moment. "Take it for a stopgap, if you wish," he advised, "but don't even think about the possibility of getting entrenched. I know a little bit about mankind, Stanley, and I'm sure that when I say I believe you are destined to have your own business and that you will never be happy or be where you belong until you get a job where you're the boss. Not that it's so important to be the big man in the company, but because you have in you what it takes to build a big enterprise." His words challenged and inspired me; I never did take the Hoover job.

But that was also the year 1936 when I would make my first advance into the silver reclaiming business. I learned of an inventor in Cleveland, Ohio, by the name of Aukerman. Immediately following World War I, Mr. Aukerman had invented a silver collector. Prior to electronic and digital photography, the Eastman Company in Rochester, New York, as well as several other film companies, manufactured photographic film out of celluloid and emulsion. Emulsion was a coating containing a high percentage of silver which was light sensitive and could retain a photographic image when submitted to brief clicks of light.

When this emulsion was mixed with developer, much of the silver was removed and fell latent to the bottom of the developing tank. With Mr. Aukerman's silver collector, this valuable metal could be reclaimed and, in my case, brought back to my little headquarters where I would refine it into commercial silver bars and put the refined silver bars on the market.

"You hit it, Stanley!" My father exulted when I told him about the invention and my plans to go to Cleveland and see the inventor about manufacturing rights. "How you fixed for startup money, son?"

"About all I've got are nickels and dimes," I replied, whereupon my father gave me $100. "This isn't a loan," he said. "It's a grant."

And so off to Cleveland I went, little realizing I had never been more centered in God's plan for my life so far as my work was concerned. The silver business would provide my heavenly Father with a venue for teaching me valued lessons that govern my life to this day.

I found Mr. Aukerman to be an elderly gentlemen with an exceptionally sharp intellect. "You're a bit young," he evaluated as he looked me over carefully. "How old are you?"

"Twenty."

It was quite obvious from the look on his face that he had hoped he could place his prized invention into more experienced hands.

"Does it work?" I asked.

"Does it work!" he laughed heartily.

"Can you demonstrate it for me?" I asked. It was a foolish question spoken in haste. I knew enough to realize it would take many weeks to actually demonstrate one of the collectors.

"You need not have the slightest qualms," the inventor insisted. "I spent many years perfecting my device."

"Are others using it now?" I asked.

"Of course," he answered as though I should have known. But when I tried to press further for details, he changed the subject. He neglected to tell me he spent nearly thirty years in the invention process.

He became quite buoyant when I asked him to show me how the collector functioned. "You see inside here," his presentation began as he tilted the unit toward me. "There's a battery in there. See those positive and negative plates?"

I nodded.

"When the unit is placed in the fixing solution of a photographic lab, these plates are activated, and the generated electricity draws the silver onto the plates. You place these units with photographers, of course, and then in due time collect them. Then the silver is smelted, refined and cleansed of its impurities."

"How much silver will the collector salvage before it needs to be smelted down?"

"Upward of $20," he replied. I cringed, having envisioned a much more substantial harvest than that.

"How long does that take?" I asked.

He hesitated.

"Months?"

He nodded and said simply, "It varies."

I would learn for myself that it took fully a year for most collectors to accomplish their reclamation.

"It depends on how busy the photo lab is," is all Mr. Aukerman would say. "Some do big businesses in portrait photography, while others maybe take a few pictures on weekends."

"What's it going to cost me to make one of these units?" I pursued further.

"They are simple, as you can see. I would judge an enterprising young go-getter like you could mass produce them for $3 or $4 each, maybe less." A salesman in his own right, the old gentleman waxed eloquent as he told me, "Twenty tons of silver is used every week in our country in the manufacturing of film, and eighty percent of it is washed out into the sewers. A hundred units, in my conservative estimate, would bring in a net amount of $10,000 to $12,000. A thousand units, once you establish your business, would collect an annual amount of over $100,000."

"Have you patented the invention?" I asked guardedly.

To which he replied without blinking an eye, "My patent's as solid as the rock of Gibraltar."

"And the patent's for sale, as I understand it."

"Not for sale, Mr. Tam," he replied, talking down to me just a bit. "But if you're interested in my unit, we can work out a contract where you pay me on a royalty basis. If you hustle, you can become a rich man in a short period of time."

I found him reasonable when we drew up the agreement, and he required no advance payment. I returned to Lima brimming with enthusiasm. The very next morning I set to work manufacturing the units with encouraging facility.

I called the units Tamco Silver Collectors. When I had thirty of the collectors made, I hit the road.

In those days, even small towns usually had at least one photographer who developed his own films. In larger towns I found photographers who had quite sophisticated establishments, including productive processing labs.

"Will you sell those collectors to me?" one photographer asked.

"They aren't for sale," I told him. "You pay a small user's fee to cover the cost of manufacturing."

"Depending if they work or not," the photographer said, "That's reasonable enough."

"They'll work like a charm," I assured him.

I had anticipated enthusiastic response to my collectors but, to the contrary, I met frequent resistance. "Can't possibly be that much silver in my business," one of the smaller photographers would say.

"Looks like more of a nuisance than anything," commented another.

But there were those who agreed to give my collectors a try, though most days they were few and far between. Even though I didn't find the market I had hoped to develop, I was able to maintain reasonable enthusiasm. Somehow, I sensed a destiny in those collectors.

I kept busy making units, but after four months had gone by, I became restless and decided to check on some of the first placements. This proved to be a harsh awakening for me. None of the collectors I checked had anywhere near sufficient silver to warrant harvesting. One thing I didn't anticipate was that my enterprise would become a veritable joke to many of the photo studios. "Hi ho silver!" someone called out to me the first time I came. I would hear it many times.

Months passed. It became increasingly difficult to convince photographers they should install my silver collectors. "What's the most any photographer has made on his royalties?" one man asked. When I started struggling for what to say, he gestured for me to leave.

At another studio the man exclaimed, "You admit you have yet to collect your first ounce of silver, yet you expect me to buy one of these little toys and place them in my developing tank. What kind of businessman would my friends think me to be if I did such a thing?"

Eventually, the collectors did their work and I began to harvest them. The first unit to be smelted down earned a gross amount of $5.

Fortunately, I set up a few labs where the owners were both patient and good-natured. They understood that I was still in the experimental process and quite willingly approved being guinea pigs.

At best, I was going steadily backward. Then came the time when, down to my last $25, I drove to Columbus to harvest collectors and try to place more units. It didn't take much mathematics to figure out what impossibility I faced at the thought of making this business succeed.

"Lord," I prayed in desperation, "how am I going to convince photographers to reclaim silver? And if I get them to do it, how will I survive the twelve months it takes for them to have anything for me to harvest?"

All too well I knew the answer to my questions. God was to put me into His school of faith. Faith is like muscle—for it to grow, it must be exercised. He has given to us at birth all the faith that we will ever need. "God hath dealt to every man the measure of faith" (Romans 12:3, KJV). Just like David, who first killed a bear, then a lion before he killed Goliath, the same happened to me.

God began guiding me step by step down the path of faith. I lost my keys at a hotel and as I was kneeling at the bed asking God to find them, I spied them under the bed as I started to get up. Traveling one day far from home, I broke an axle at 10 o'clock at night. The temperature had suddenly gone to zero. I had no coat, and searching for shelter, I saw a light in the distance. The man said that he had left the light in the window before retiring for his brother who had gone to town. Another time, I ran out of gasoline on the highway at 1 o'clock in the morning, the temperature 16 degrees below zero, and there was no anti-freeze in my radiator. I had to drain the water out immediately. God provided a kind farmer who put me up for the night and towed my car the next morning to a filling station. God was preparing me for the Goliaths in the future, but I didn't know it at the time.

So one afternoon, walking down the street in Columbus, I made a decision. "Lord," I mulled, "I quit." With that, I headed homeward, my heart aching, my mind clambering with confusion, as I drove up Highway 23 bound for Lima.

"Lord," I prayed, "it seemed so sure I was following Your guidance, that it was because of You I learned about Mr. Auckerman. What am I going to do? How can I ever go back to calling on farmers and ringing doorbells?"

In that next moment I had a startling experience. It would happen many times in the future, becoming a phenomenon which I have learned to anticipate and greatly cherish. I felt absolutely sure I sensed God speaking to me. "It doesn't need to be a disappointment, Stanley," I heard Him say. "You don't have to go broke."

"But you can see what's happening, God." I lamented. "Maybe if I had some capital, I could keep going. But I'm down to my last dollars. I can't keep going."

"You shouldn't be concerned about lack of finances. All you need is faith in Me," the inner voice continued.

"I do have faith, Lord."

"Enough to turn your business over to Me? To let Me run it for you?" A hushed awe came over me. I was serious about my Christian life. I wanted God first in everything. With the thought of actually depending on Him to run my business, I couldn't quite rationalize it in my thinking.

"Lord," I prayed, slowly, deliberately, aloud. "Could this really be? I want it if it's possible. I will turn my business over to you. Take it, Lord, and if You'll make it succeed, I'll honor You in every way I can. I promise!" A surge of assurance came to my heart as I prayed those words.

Arriving back in Lima, I told my parents what had happened. Though unbelievers, they responded with wide eyes.

"That's wonderful," my dad said. "I wish you all the luck in the world, son."

Then I did something I shouldn't have done. But I did it in innocence. I asked my dad if he could help me with the money I would need. "I'm asking for a loan, Dad," I told him, "not a gift." He gave me $12, saying, "I haven't got another dime I can spare."

It was the last time I would borrow a dollar from anybody. With God in charge of my business, I would only have to ask Him for economic sustenance. I would not so much as darken the door of a bank, except to make deposits.

I would rest on the promise of Philippians 4:19: "My God shall supply all your need according to His riches in glory by Christ Jesus" (NKJV).

THIRTEEN

Needs Supplied, Wants Granted

That roadside decision north of our Ohio state capital—when, in my faltering faith, I turned my business over to God—became decisive in my life. No doubt struggling very similarly to the way I had done, four others had tried to build a silver reclaiming business and had gone bankrupt. Were it not for the sovereign will of God, I would have been number five. But I wasn't.

Can you imagine it? There I was, a young aspirant newly turned of age. I had no capital. My product required a twelve-month turnover from the time I placed a collector in a photo studio laboratory until I was smelting the scarce harvest of silver in a barely adequate furnace.

But, despite those apparent obstacles, I knew I could do it—God had told me so!

Making a go of it? I tell you, friend, when you commit yourself to God and begin learning how to trust the promises He gives you in the Bible, you launch yourself on a spiritual voyage during which you may experience the winds of adversity coming from all directions but the sure hand of God is always there, sustaining and guiding you. I wouldn't trade those experiences for the affluence of the richest men on earth.

Take, for example, the time I made my way across Ohio into northern Kentucky. All along my route, I checked photo labs in the hopes of gathering several silver-laden collectors ready for me to take home to my little furnace.

You see, I had added a modest markup of a couple of dollars to each collector in addition to factoring in the cost of manufacturing. So if I could place a reasonable number of the silver collectors, I could obtain sufficient cash flow to sustain my struggling enterprise. Unfortunately, the trip turned out to be very discouraging.

As I neared Athens, Ohio, I remembered something. On a visit to the country school church I attended as a boy, I heard someone mention a Pastor Huff who had pastored the church when I was a boy. I was told he now occupied a little church near the town of Athens. I thought it would be pleasant to look him up so I could tell him of my conversion and have some fellowship with him. But I was so discouraged, I proceeded on into town instead of looking him up. For my first stop, I visited a photographer who had called telling me he had removed his collector from his processing tank. I had tried to convince him otherwise but he wouldn't budge, so I removed his collector and crossed him off my list.

There were several other photographers I needed to see, but it was getting late in the afternoon, and I was in a very down mood. I tended to be in a discouraged mood as I looked for a place to stay the night. I had barely enough money for an inexpensive room and to get me back to Lima the following day, so I chose a low-priced hotel. I did not realize my room would be one of the murkiest available in the state of Ohio.

I stumbled into that room and flopped onto the bed and then down to my knees. "Well, here we go again," I prayed. "The business still belongs to You, Lord, and has less and less value every day I struggle to keep it going."

There was a Gideon Bible in the room. I opened it to Philippians 4:19 just to assure myself it was still there. I did a lot of thinking that night. I would have thrown in the towel for sure had it not been for the Columbus experience when the Lord so distinctly told me I could turn the business over to Him.

I thought about something else that night too. "Lord," I prayed aloud, staring up into the darkness, "isn't it about time for You to bring that special person into my life? Will You maybe find her for me soon?"

I laughed out loud! What sense was it for me to ask the Lord for a wife when I scarcely had enough money to cover the cost of a few tanks of gas?

The next morning, I bought a couple of doughnuts for my breakfast and visited a few photographers around town—without so much as a dime's worth of business. Finally, at about 10 o'clock, I was so discouraged that I got into my car and headed for home. I had 78 cents in my pocket and home was about 160 miles away.

After I had gone about ten miles, calamity struck. The motor of my car began to knock, and I knew that a rod was about to go out. I managed to make it to a town called Chauncey. I stopped in the heart of that little town where two roads crossed. I pulled over to the side of the street, bowed my head over the steering wheel of my car and prayed, "Lord, this is the end of the streetcar track. I am discouraged, broke and 160 miles from home. You have to take over. I am at a crossroads, do I give up this business or do I go on? You make the decision." When I looked up, I saw a garage on the corner of the crossroads. I walked over to the garage and met the mechanic and told him, "I just burned out the rod in my car. What would you charge me to fix it?"

He said, "Twelve dollars."

I said, "I have 78 cents."

He asked, "Where are you from?"

I said, "Lima, Ohio."

He said that was too far away to extend credit. He went back to his work. I just stood there. Pretty soon he came back to me. "I'll tell you what you could do," the mechanic offered. I'm convinced it was the Lord who interceded in that man's mind. "See the high school up on the hill? They have a mechanics class and are always looking for cars to fix. They don't charge a dime."

In that same moment, I was back in my car and heading out to the highway, sounding more like an armored vehicle going into battle than an automobile plunging on its way. Once I reached the school, I found the mechanics teacher and convinced him to come out and listen to my engine.

"We won't know how bad it is until we get into the engine," he said, "but it's obviously a rod going out."

"Then you'll fix it for me?" I asked eagerly.

"Yes, we will find a used rod in the junk around here, but you'll have to pay for any parts," he added.

I told him my story, even a hint of my having given my business to the Lord. He listened openly and believed me.

"I will get my boys right on your car, but there is one other problem."

"What's that?"

"We won't be able to get at it until tomorrow."

My heart sank. "Can you take care of this little matter, too, Lord?" I prayed.

And instantly I had my answer. Pastor Huff! The clergyman who had pastored our little church years back! I could leave the car at the school, hitchhike to Pastor Huff's little town and ask him for a night's lodging, which I did. It brought tears to Pastor Huff's eyes when I told him of my conversion, and especially when I detailed for him the way in which I had turned my business over to God.

That night, as I stretched out onto a comfortable bed, my heart was like a fountain of praise.

"It seems like You turn everything that happens to me into something good. I praise you for that, Lord." Then, as part of my prayer and yet in a moment of wonderment I added, "It makes me wonder, what will You do next in my life?"

In the years to come, my thoughts often went back to that experience at the crossroads in the little town of Chauncey. It was one of the crossroads in my life. What if I had given up, quit the business, gotten a job? United States Plastic would never had been born—God's business, whose profits support almost 1,000 missionaries on the mission field today.

My advice to you is, don't give up, give it to God.

CHAPTER

FOURTEEN

The Girl from Rockford

I had girl friends. Dates, however, consisted primarily of escorting someone to an event. Nothing more, no matter how bright the moon or fragrant the roses and lilacs. I believed God had someone in His plan for me, and so I had no time for exploratory affairs. God, who was leading me day by day in such distinct evidences of His guidance would, I was convinced, bring into my life the girl He wanted me to marry. He would do it in His time and in His way.

But though I was very serious in my prayers for a wife, foremost in my requests to God were that I might succeed in business. As I look back now, I realize I didn't fully understand what that meant. I didn't realize my wife and I would be able to give millions of dollars through the years to the Lord's work. It continued to be a long, hard road, yet I seemed to have been inoculated against all-out discouragement, no matter how lean some of the months might be.

I had a promise from God. If I turned the business over to Him, He would make it succeed. Four others before me had tried and failed. That didn't matter. I had God's promise!

I had pretty much covered Ohio and Kentucky, placing silver collectors in many of the photo laboratories there, so I began working westward, largely avoiding Chicago because I felt so much more comfortable in smaller communities. I ventured along the southern section of Wisconsin, then down into northern Illinois, eventually checking out Rockford.

The money I earned placing silver collectors in Rockford Photo Labs was a mere pittance compared to the great treasure God had waiting for me there. Her name was Juanita—Juanita Lindeman.

She had become a believer at the age of eight and, in the large Evangelical Free Church of that city, not only learned about the 7,480 promises in the Bible, but that He could make these promises integral to her own life. As a consequence, growing up for her included the development of a lasting commitment to Christ as her Savior and Lord. She remained the zestful, personable and lovely young lady I would know her to be but with the added distinction of a devout lifestyle.

The Rockford Free Church emphasized foreign missions, and sent scores of workers out into the mission fields of the world. Juanita gave many serious thoughts to becoming one of their number. She was made of more quality stuff than simply to play follow-the-leader, even in a spiritual sense. If she were to become a missionary, she would want God to speak with her personally about it, making His call distinct and assuring.

Of course, many Rockford young people did not respond to a missionary call. In Juanita's case, however, she had many of the personal attributes one expects to find in a missionary.

As we look back over the earlier years of our lives, both of us can see how God prepared the two of us strategically and specifically for service together in a unique form of world outreach. Her analytical mind, secretarial skills and ability to organize her work, added to a warm and gregarious personality, all proved to be attributes the Lord would use in making her the kind of lay person whose entire focus is on the world and its need for the gospel.

Juanita discovered a unique method of prayer by weaving the Scriptures into her intercession. One of her favorite prayer reinforcements in the Scriptures was Proverbs 3:6: "In all thy ways acknowledge him, and he shall direct thy paths" (KJV).

Kneeling alone in her room, she developed an intimate relationship with her Heavenly Father, weaving Scripture into her prayers and saying, "This is what You promise to do in Your Word, Lord, and I trust You to keep Your promises."

It was an inspiring moment when she told me how she made a point of talking to her Heavenly Father as intimately as to her earthly father.

Her prayers became more frequent and intense early in 1937. She had been going with a young fellow named Ed and had thought of matrimony. Then they had a series of disagreements and she broke off the relationship.

One early summer evening, while walking to a friend's house nearby to assist in preparing decorations for a Memorial Day event being staged by the young people, she was besieged with serious thoughts and made this request. "Lord, You know how lonely I've been since breaking up with Ed. Will You send someone for me to meet who loves You with all his heart? Someone good-looking and different." An event which occurred several months earlier lingered in her thoughts. That memory coincided with a weekend on my own schedule.

I had been venturing in a territory well beyond Lima in my efforts to place silver collectors. This included northern Illinois and southern Wisconsin, as I mentioned earlier, and involved my wanting to some day venture down into Rockford, Illinois, a place that always caught my eye when I scanned highway maps. Finally, in the summer of 1937, the opportunity came. I was excited about the new clients I might obtain but, as I indicated previously, I had no clue as to what a landmark Rockford was to become for the remainder of my life.

I had been working in southern Wisconsin and, for some reason, kept thinking about Rockford, which was just a few miles below the border. It had not been an especially good week and I thought I should head back to Lima either Friday night or first thing Saturday morning.

I checked out Janesville and on down to Beloit, both towns yielding marginal results, so my spirits should have been a bit low. Instead I had a sense of victory in my heart engendered by the Lord's guidance. I nonchalantly looked at the map, saw that it was approximately twenty miles down Highway 51 from Beloit to Rockford, so I decided to at least go down for a Saturday to look around.

I was impressed with how attractive I found Rockford to be, with its broad boulevards, lovely homes and a profusion of trees, flowers and well-tended lawns. Actually, as I mentioned when I was still up in Wisconsin, I needed to be heading back to Lima and save Rockford for another time but, as I drove through, I told myself I wasn't in all that big of a hurry so I decided to make a reconnaissance tour of the place with future business stops in mind.

Then, too, I never used Sunday for sleeping in when I took those road trips. Always I looked for a place to worship. Surely, I thought, Rockford would have some excellent churches, being such an attractive place.

So, Saturday afternoon, I drove around the city, making note of places I would be visiting in the future. My Saturday search did not reward me as readily as I thought it might. Then, turning onto Seventh Street, my eyes caught the large display of a sign outside a church: "CHRIST DIED FOR OUR SINS."

My heart warmed instantly. Driving closer, I saw the name of the church, Swedish Free Church.

Swedish Free? I pondered. *Must be a denomination of some sort*, I told myself, because it was obviously evangelical and was quite a large edifice. I puzzled over that "Swedish" name. Did it mean Sunday services were conducted in the Swedish language? I didn't know a whisper of Swedish.

But then I noted again the words, "CHRIST DIED FOR OUR SINS," in plain English. I was sufficiently curious to decide I would attend.

Next morning I knew exactly where I wanted to go, having checked out the terrain so thoroughly the day before. So I headed down Charles Street toward Seventh, arriving at the Swedish Free Church as though I had done it a dozen times before—not realizing, of course, I would do it dozens of times in the future.

A tinge of excitement quickened my pulse as I stood for a moment to survey the surroundings. Several people passed me. Two older members greeted each other and conversed busily in the Swedish language.

I entered. A personable young man by the name of Bob Miller met me within seconds after I entered the door. One of the prominent young leaders of the youth society had been killed in a tragic accident, he explained, so usual hospitality might be somewhat modified. To the contrary, I found myself surrounded by the welcoming warmth of young people such as I had rarely encountered before.

Bob and I sat together during the morning service, and, following the benediction, he turned and asked, "What's your schedule for this afternoon?"

"Get back to the hotel for an hour or so," I replied. "Been pushing myself all week and I'm just a mite sleepy."

"That sounds like a good agenda item for me too," Bob said. "Do you think you'll sack out all afternoon?"

"No, only for an hour or so."

Whatever Bob had in mind I was sure would be worthwhile, so I wanted to be available. What he had in mind was a memorial service back at the church, with young people coming from all over the state to honor this leader who had been so abruptly taken from them. "This fellow was our district youth society chairman," Bob informed me.

"When do you want me ready?" I asked.

"Can you make it at 3 o'clock?"

We agreed on the time and I met him there. I was intensely moved by the memorial service. Sitting there, listening to all this fellow—his name was Hilding Ahlstrom, I remember—had accomplished was itself a ministration to my heart.

"Makes me feel like a turtle walking backward," I whispered to my new friend.

"That's two of us," Bob responded.

Hilding, a student at Wheaton College, was on his way to a National Youth Conference of the Evangelical Free Church in California when he was killed in a tragic car accident. Hilding Ahlstrom, I subsequently learned, and Juanita Lindeman had been second cousins.

It was a meaningful time in my life, setting the stage for what was about to transpire. At the close of the memorial service, the emcee announced that all out-of-town visitors were invited to be dinner guests at a downtown restaurant.

"You're from out of town," Bob turned to me and said, a pleased grin coming across his face. "You qualify."

A large group attended the dinner. My old shyness syndrome reared its ugly head, so I tended to isolate myself. Bob, realizing I had some social weaknesses to overcome, gave me space. However, he did ask if I would give my testimony. This was something I could do with increasing liberty, so I readily agreed.

I gave a résumé of the Tamco Company and a quick overview of the unique procedure of silver collectors. Somehow, I caught the attention of those sitting at the restaurant tables. I told about the farm lady who had led me to Christ, how disappointed I had been as a salesman but that I was learning how to let God take control of my work.

I was becoming aware of something important, even that early in my career. People, even young people, reacted with immediate interest to my telling about giving God control of my business. Several came to me after the program was dismissed, commending me for my decision.

As I stood there chatting, my eyes turned away momentarily from the group, catching a glance from a wholesome, very pretty young woman who was about my age. We looked fully at each other for just that one moment, then both turned away.

Bob, having seen the brief event, touched my arm and moved me over to the young lady, introducing us. I remember my ears glowing, my cheeks blushing, my pulse doing a drum roll. Before I could manage just a sputtering of words, someone called to the young lady and she excused herself and was gone.

I made a few more trips to Rockford in the following months, but only on weekdays so I didn't get back to the church right away. I did, however, take a couple of drives past Seventh Street and the Swedish Free Church edifice.

Juanita Lindeman. The name was—and still is—indelible upon my mind.

I told myself I must schedule a weekend so I could attend services and meet my new friends once more—especially Juanita!

Then came that evening, a year later, when Juanita went to a friend's house to help prepare decorations for the youth retreat over Memorial Day at a summer camp. She had a demanding executive secretarial job, which often left her weary at the end of the day. This was one such day, and she entered into the activities with enthusiasm, but also kept looking at the clock to see when she needed to get home for a recuperative night's rest.

By late evening, they had their handiwork completed. "I've got a very heavy day coming at work tomorrow," she told her girlfriend, "so I'd better be heading back home."

They heard a loud knock at the door. Juanita's friend answered it. It was Bob Miller and beside him a friend from out of town.

Juanita busied herself clearing the table on which she had been working, when her friend returned and said, "It's Bob Miller, Juanita. He has a friend from out of town. Bob and his girl wondered if you'd like to double with them."

Juanita glanced at her watch. "It's 11 o'clock," she said. "I've really got to get to sleep." But she added, "Who is this guy?"

"He's a salesman from Ohio."

Juanita put her hands on her hips. A flare of resentment touched her countenance. "Now wait a minute!" she jibed. "I'm not the kind who goes out on blind dates with strange salesmen."

"You've met him, Juanita. He's been to our church."

"Met him? What's his name?"

"Stanley Tam."

"Tell Bob I'll be right there!"

FIFTEEN

Old-Fashioned Romance

I believe in old-fashioned romance—with all my heart. I believe in a relationship that honors the Lord in every detail from sitting together in church to being in a parked car at some secluded rendezvous.

Granted, the Bible doesn't give young people specifics on the subject of romance and courtship, yet the principles are as clear as the print on its pages. The Bible ascends to some of its finest eloquence in Proverbs 30:18-19,

> There be three things which are too wonderful for me, yea, four which I know not: The way of an eagle in the air; the way of a serpent upon a rock; the way of a ship in the midst of the sea; and the way of a man with a maid. (KJV)

That way is clarified in Psalm 119:9, "Wherewithal shall a young man cleanse his way? by taking heed thereto according to thy word" (KJV). It is underscored by First Corinthians 10:31, "Whether therefore ye eat, or drink, or whatsoever ye do, do all to the glory of God" (KJV). It is sanctified in Romans 12:1, "I beseech you therefore, brethren, by the mercies of God, that ye present your bodies a living sacrifice, holy, acceptable unto God, which is your reasonable service" (KJV). And put into living practice in First Corinthians 3:9, "We are labourers together with God" (KJV).

I arranged frequent trips into the Rockford area even though it was 300 miles from Lima to my girlfriend's doorstep. Juanita filled in my absences with profuse correspondence, to which I responded quite often.

When I did come, we had our favorite "parking" spots, several of them along the banks of the broad and boisterous Rock River which flowed through the city. Juanita was always full of chatter about Rockford, the church and her job. I relished every word of it. She also wanted to know about my work, how my sales were progressing, sensing with me my own keenness of involvement in my successes and my difficult times.

Ordinarily, bashfulness should have smitten me at each renewal of our togetherness. Thankfully, however, Juanita brimmed with self-confidence and was blessed with abundant social skills which gave an endearing winsomeness to her personality. She seemed to have a special talent for putting me at ease.

I thrived on the way we talked about things of the Lord, the way we both wanted Him to guide our lives. I had no doubt of the Lord's sovereignty in bringing us together. "I knew when I first met her," I told my friends back in Lima, "that she was someone God had picked out for me to marry."

Then one night when I checked into a hotel, I got to thinking. What about that account in the Bible where Gideon put out a fleece to be absolutely sure of God's intentions for him?

"A fleece!" I exclaimed aloud. Wouldn't it be beautiful to have the Lord show me, even as He showed Gideon, the certainty of His plan? So, before retiring, I partially opened the window of my hotel room and pushed a dry wash cloth onto the windowsill.

"Lord," I prayed, "if Juanita is to be my wife, make this washcloth soaking wet in the morning."

There was no rain during the night, seemingly no heavy dew in the morning. As I quickly rolled out of bed I hurried to the window. The wash cloth was as dry as it was when I placed it there the previous evening. The thought of that washcloth troubled me all during the day. Was it possible that I could feel so sure of something, having prayed and prayed for the Lord's guidance, and then put it to a biblical test and find I was wrong?

I made very few productive contacts during that day, so heavy was my mind with concern for what had happened. But then I thought of something. Perhaps the Lord was only testing me. Just as Gideon had, I would make another test. So that night I soaked the washcloth, and placed it sopping wet on the windowsill. "Lord," I prayed. "Please make this washcloth totally dry by morning, if it is Your will for me to marry Juanita."

I had a restless night, almost getting up a couple of times to make an advanced check on the wet cloth. At the crack of dawn I was up, rushing over to the window for inspection. My heart sank. The washcloth remained soaking wet!

Right then and there I decided fleeces were a special arrangement God had with Gideon. The fleece test had nothing whatever to do with me and my relationship to the lovely lady in Rockford!

I told Juanita nothing about the fleece test.

Back to Rockford I went, again and again, as our relationship deepened.

One night I took her hand and said, "I feel He has guided our lives." There was sufficient moonlight so we could look deeply into each other's eyes.

"Has and is," Juanita said.

With her inoffensive frankness and openness, she asked if I had had many girlfriends since graduating from high school. "You could hardly call them girlfriends," I replied awkwardly. "They would go with me places and things like that, but they were more just friends than girlfriends." Awkwardly I added, "The only thing that attracted girls to me was my car."

I wanted to ask her about boyfriends but my tongue went thick in my mouth.

She told me she had had several boyfriends. "The last fellow I met and dated was named Ed." My heart sank. I wondered if this Ed and I were competitors. Juanita quickly caught my concern and said, "Oh, he's out of the picture now. He lives and has a job in Minneapolis, same distance from here as Lima." She opened her mouth as though to speak further, but refrained.

"You, uh," I stammered awkwardly, "this Ed guy, you, uh?"

"We broke up just before you and I met," she replied quietly.

Excitement and tranquility coursed through my body in a delighting burst. Happiness and relief. Had it not been for my retiring ways, I might well have proposed to that dear person at that moment. The moon had come up full, giving touches of diamond sparkle to the water of the river as it coursed past us. A moment for potential romance, to be sure, but something about the softness of night light and the gathering tenderness of our feelings for each other also awakened our desire to share with each other gems of blessing and guidance we had found in the Scriptures since our last meeting. The closer we came to each other emotionally, the more intensely our spiritual rapport developed.

I cherished her telling me how much the Bible related to her as a person. "Many times," she said, "when I read the Bible, especially when I'm searching for a special answer to some need, it's as though the words on the page become God's voice speaking to me."

My pulse quickened.

"This happened particularly with the Psalms," she told me. "I'm learning how to have a deepening relationship with the Lord that relates to Bible promises and my prayers. Sometimes I spend an hour or more 'praying through the Psalms' as I call it. Most of the Psalms are prayers, don't you think?"

"I think so," I said, admitting to myself I did not yet have this kind of intimacy with the Scriptures.

Juanita would read aloud one of her favorite places in the Psalms, the second to last verse of Psalm 139: "Search me, O God and know my heart," allowing the text to become the voice of her prayer to God. "Try me and know my thoughts" (KJV).

She grew quiet, looking out at the river. "Often, when I use this psalm for prayer," she said in a near whisper, "it is as though I can feel the Holy Spirit deep down inside me, doing exactly what I have prayed."

"That's fantastic," was all I could say. I listened with intent silence, as this dear person proceeded to tell me about her experiences in prayer. *Who needs fleece?* my heart cried out in eloquent silence.

If seemingly insurmountable challenges confronted her, she would turn to Philippians 4:13: "I can do all things through Christ who strengthens me" (NKJV).

Often at night, when out on sales trips, I would stretch out on my bed in a cheap hotel and imagine it became like a lavish chamber in the royal quarters of the King of Kings.

"Are you giving Juanita to me, Lord?" I would pray. "Are you preparing me for her, just as you are also preparing her for me?"

I would switch on the light, take the Gideon Bible and, as Juanita often did, browse the Psalms for promises. There I would find those promises, such as Psalm 84:11: "For the LORD God is a sun and shield: the LORD will give grace and glory: no good thing will he withhold from them that walk uprightly" (KJV).

Three months after we met on that initial blind date, shyness in her presence was a thing of the past. On one of my visits, she prepared a tasty picnic and we drove to Sinissippi Park as the sun hung wearily against the western sky.

"The food is delicious," I complimented, "and I'm starved."

She looked across the park table to me in nonverbal eloquence, her lovely dimples and soft, searching eyes reacting to my commendation.

Ordinarily I should have been stricken to silence by such an exuberant person. I had never cared for people, girls especially, who chattered profusely about incidentals. There was no accusing Juanita on that score, however. She liked to talk about witness opportunities, about blessings she gleaned from the Bible, about prayers she had seen answered.

"Tell me about your day," she broke off abruptly.

It was the opportunity for which I had been waiting. I told her that I had been enjoying quite good business of late—so good, in fact, I had began thinking seriously about some things. She looked at me, her eyes widening.

"What things?" she asked.

I hesitated another moment, my courage waning just a mite. This was entirely new territory for my emotions. Then I got up and walked around to the other side of the table so I could sit beside her. "Business is good enough," I began, carefully articulating each word, "so I can begin to think about getting married."

I inched closer to her and she inched toward me.

"I want you to be the one I marry," I managed to say. "Will you, Juanita?"

"Gladly," she responded.

We closed the distance between us. We kissed. Our very first.

Yes, ours was an old-fashioned romance. I wouldn't have had it any other way. Nor would my lady. Above all, that's the kind of premarital relationship which allows room for the Lord to mold two people together in partnership with Him as well as with each other.

Juanita Lindeman and Stanley Tam were married on January 21, 1939 at the Rockford, Illinois, Evangelical Free Church.

We parked our first home, this small house trailer, beside a gas station in Peru, Illinois, for 50 cents a night, including power and restroom privileges.

Several years later, in 1946, we began to melt silver that had been reclaimed from photographic solution. From this crucible holding 250 pounds, we poured 25-pound silver bars.

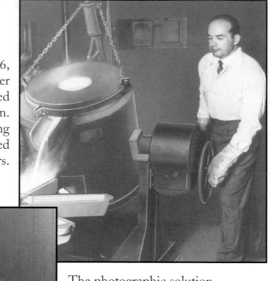

The photographic solution was supplied from 10,000 customers—photographers and medical facility x-ray departments.

We placed a gospel tract in every shipment. In 2001, the shipments totaled about 150,000.

Our first factory, established in 1944, was on Victory Street in Lima, Ohio.

Family photo, top row L to R: Darrell Long, Kristin Lytle, Stuart Long, Jennifer McNiven, Sarah Long, Mary MacDonald (friend from London, England). Second row L to R: Wes Lytle, Prudence Long, Michele Von Tobel, Jack Williams, Rachel Williams, R. Stanley Tam, Paul Von Tobel IV, Paul Von Tobel III. First row L to R: Becky Lytle, Stanley Long, Heather Williams, Heather Ann Williams, Bryan Williams, Ethel Williams, Juanita Tam, Peter Von Tobel, Candy Von Tobel.

My wife, Juanita (center) poses with our four daughters.
L to R: Prudence Long, Becky Lytle, Candy Von Tobel, Rachel Williams

Juanita's hobby, china painting, provides
many beautiful gifts for family and friends.

We have devotions together every morning at breakfast,
a habit we have faithfully kept since we were married in 1939.

Sixty-two years have passed since God and I founded United States
Plastics. Four businesses are housed under a five-acre roof: States
Smelting and Refining Company, United States Plastic Corporation,
Tamco Industries and Industrial Safety Company.

Wes Lytle, my son-in-law, is now president of all the companies. Every Saturday, when possible, we have lunch together—a Whopper® for each of us!

Then Wes and I go to the factory to check out current projects and dream and plan for the future.

My friend, Art Arthur, and I have been prayer partners for thirty-eight years. When we're in town, we meet every Thursday to pray in Art's car at a city park.

In June of 1979, I received an Honorary Doctor of Humane Letters (L.H.D.) award from Dr. Dennis Kinlaw, president of Asbury College.

In appreciation for contributions we made to further evangelism in Korea, Mr. Kim Yong Nae, Minister of Government Administration, awarded me a marble plaque on behalf of the Mayor of Seoul.

I had the privilege to speak through an interpreter in the largest church in the world, the Assembly of God in Seoul where Dr. Cho is the pastor.

In Bristol, England, Juanita and I knelt at the grave site of George Müller. It was through Müller's influence that I decided never to borrow money personally or for the business.

I loved to play with my daughters. Here Becky stands on my hands and Prudence (Prudy) is trying to put a pillow under my head.

My oldest daughter, Rachel Williams, holds her grandchildren (our great grandchildren), Aubry and Jack.

Candy (Von Tobel), our youngest daughter, sits astride Barney, her first horse. Candy wanted to go somewhere I thought was inappropriate, so I bribed her not to go by buying her a horse. Now in her fifties, she owns two horses and still loves to ride.

At a photographers' trade show in Chicago around 1946, we sold silver collectors. It has been our practice to have a display at every annual convention of The Photo Finishers, Photographers and X-ray Technicians.

Our granddaughter, Jennifer Lytle, with her husband, Chris McNiven.

Mildred, left, and Evelyn, right, are my two sisters. I was the middle child. We were raised on a farm with no electricity or running water. Photo taken about 1970.

These bronze plaques grace the outside wall of the factory office. They are a visual reminder and testimony to all who enter that God owns all, that we are only trustees, that we receive it from His hands and it goes back to Him.

I was presented this gold Olympiad medal from the mayor of Seoul in 1988 in appreciation for the millions of dollars that our company has donated to church planting in South Korea.

These maps of Indonesia and South Korea indicate the locations where the Every Creature Crusade has planted churches. The mission now serves in 29 countries with over 1,000 nationals involved. In 2001, they reported 84,000 decisions for Christ and 125 new churches planted.

In 1989, Juanita and I had the privilege of speaking in a Korean church with Rev. Paul Kim as the interpreter. This was my sixth trip to Korea.

This plaque was received from Asbury College when I retired
from the Board. Dr. Kinlaw, shown here with his wife, Elise,
is one of the three most influential men in my life.

Juanita and I attend the Cable Road Alliance Church
in Lima, Ohio. The congregation presented me with a
plaque making me "Elder for Life with Vote." On my left is
Pastor Keith McKnight, and to my right, the district superintendent,
Rev. C. David Mangham, Sr., Wes Lytle and Dick Spicker.

I was invited to speak at a Christian Businessmen's Association meeting in Madras, India, with well over 1,000 in attendance. I had gone there to celebrate the 25th anniversary of the Every Creature Crusade in India where we have over fifty teams of six men working. Seated far left is Rev. J.B. Crouse, President of OMS International, and next to me (R) is Bishop Dr. Ezra Sargunam.

One of the enjoyable things about being a guest in South Korea is being presented with these gorgeous leis. United States Plastic has planted more than 750 churches there.

My "retiral" business is the Tam-O-Shanter Manufacturing Co. where we manufacture Queen Anne and Chippendale style furniture. We are expanding into other wood products as the demand increases.

In 1955, when I returned from South America after turning the entire business over to the Lord, God said, "Build a new factory four times larger than the present one" (the Elida Road location). We did that, and in 1960 expanded into plastics. In 1977, we outgrew our old landlocked factory, so we started over with this new five-acre-under-one-roof factory on I-75 at Neubrecht Road. To God be the glory!

CHAPTER

SIXTEEN

Honeymoon Business Trip

We were married on Saturday, January 21, 1939—eight months following our first meeting.

Speaking facetiously for a moment, it appeared we needed to delay the marriage until spring, so we could have a lawn wedding. The reason was that I had invited Paul Klein to be my best man.

"Please get yourself a new black suit," I told him.

"I'd do it in a minute if I could," Paul replied, a look of distress spreading like a shadow across his countenance. "My problem is I just bought a suit and can't afford two in a row."

"What color is your new suit?" I asked.

"Green," he said.

I went into the same store and bought a green suit for myself, matching Paul's. The rest of the men in the wedding party followed with green suits.

When I told Juanita, she first thought I was teasing. Then, realizing the true situation, she tried to hold her poise but became quite distraught. But, in her usual practical manner, soon accepted things as they were.

Juanita and her host of friends decorated the Rockford Free Church modestly but beautifully. When I made my entry down the long church aisle, I felt like a king ascending to his throne. Moments later, when my sweetheart stood beside me, the reality of that time came clearly to my mind.

It was not a matter of simply getting married. It was a moment as sacred and definitive as that evening when I pulled up alongside a road outside of Columbus and received the Lord's assurance that, if I would turn my business over to Him, He would deliver it from the threat of bankruptcy and make it prosper. Now here was the helpmate He had provided for me. Together, we would see His promise fulfilled.

Outside, a lazy blanket of snow filtered downward, adding to the solemnity and unalloyed sacredness of the ceremony. It was a picture-perfect setting, an event programed in heaven. According to my bride, I smiled through the entire ceremony.

"I'd never seen teeth so white," she told me afterward. "I don't suppose you can fall in love with a smile, but it certainly can intensify what's already in your heart."

Pastor Elmer Johnson, one of the Free Church's most prominent clergyman, conducted the ceremony. He had a warm smile of his own throughout the ceremony, enhancing the magnitude of the occasion.

I had an uncle who built house trailers, better known as RVs today. Adhering to my policy of no-credit purchasing, I had saved $500, exactly the price my uncle would have charged anyone other than myself who might have purchased it.

With my Chevrolet, I took the prestigious eighteen-foot trailer on practice runs around the streets of Rockford, catching the attention of onlookers wherever I drove.

I was so sure God intended Juanita to be my wife that I had my uncle begin building it even before I proposed. Juanita squealed with delight when I gave her a quick look. "Oh, Stanley," she exclaimed, "we're beginning our life together in deluxe fashion!" It was avant-garde, state-of-the-art, you name it. A double bed pulled out of the wall, it had a breakfast nook, camp stove, cupboards and even a bathroom of sorts. I envisioned myself pleased as a maharaja carrying his bride away from her childhood residence on a royally jeweled behemoth.

About 8 o'clock, Juanita and I slipped away from the reception and went hastily to our car and trailer. Parked in the light of a bright street lamp, we could plainly see how our house on wheels had been festooned with ribbons and bric-a-brac.

Our 1936 Chevy, towing the palace-on-wheels, moved elegantly along Rockford streets and onto highway 251 heading south as we honeymooned toward less winter climes. The snowfall continued, causing the roads to become somewhat slick, and I drove with care because I hadn't had a chance to give the trailer a practice run under such conditions.

We passed through a couple of small towns on our way toward Rochelle. On and on we drove, then entered the outskirts of another small village.

"Where are we staying tonight?" Juanita wondered.

"I've got a hunch, sweetheart," I replied.

"Like what?"

"Watch me." With that, I did a right turn into a gas station, pulled up to the pumps where, in those days, there was no such thing as self-service.

"Fill 'er up," I said as I stepped out for a stretch.

"That's quite an impressive trailer you're towing," the proprietor said as he expedited my request. He took a step back for a better view of the trailer. "Where do you park this thing nights?" he asked.

"When do you close?" I queried.

"In ten minutes."

"If you agree to the idea," I said cautiously, "How much would you charge to let us hook up to your electricity and use your toilet facilities for the night?"

"Say, now," he brightened, "there's a possible new angle for our business!"

"You'll do it?" I asked.

"Sure," he replied, "for a buck."

Had we made it to Niagra Falls, or nested in the valley land of some utopian Shangri-la, we could not possibly have been happier. United as man and wife, we had also affirmed a spiritual partnership which would endure forever.

Among our many golden memories will always be our first morning together. Juanita with her Bible, and I with mine, we sat face-to-face in our mealtime nook as we took turns reading the Word of God together.

From my Bible: "Husbands, love your wives, even as Christ also loved the church, and gave himself for it" (Ephesians 5:25, KJV).

From my bride's Bible: "I am my beloved's, and his desire is toward me. Come, my beloved, let us go forth into the field; let us lodge in the villages. Let us get up early to the vineyards; let us see if the vine flourish, whether the tender grapes appear, and the pomegranates bud forth" (Song of Solomon 7:10-12, KJV).

We both prayed, thanking God for bringing us together, for the harmony we knew He was going to give us in our marriage and our ministry. My confidence in the Scriptures increased as together we experienced the dimension of the Bible ministering to both of us simultaneously.

That was the inauguration of our family worship, which continues to this day. We were happy on our honeymoon, content in our home on wheels. My lady had a continuous smile on her lips, and often a song issued forth as she went about her duties onboard. I had eaten her food before, but never in continuity as was the case now. For sheer economy, we ate all our meals onboard. But saving money was not the only reason. Juanita was an imaginative cook, with as many menus in her heart as in her head. She included variety and those tasty touches only a woman of sophisticated culinary skills can give to a meal.

"I've eaten in a lot of restaurants, sweetheart," I told her, "but I can't think of a one that ever came up to your standard."

It amazed me how many different things she could do with a potato, how she could gather the trimmings from a day's outgo of vegetables and concoct a soup which was a delicacy all on its own.

With her own money, she purchased knick-knacks, which added much to the trailer's attractive interior.

There was little opportunity to open charge accounts in those days, but even so, I made it clear that ours was a pay-as-you-go marriage. When Juanita lightly disputed, I placed my hand on her shoulders and looked fully into her eyes and said, "Sweetheart, we're in business with God. We pay cash for everything. How else can we experience the promises of God in every detail of our lives?"

At the beginning, Juanita resisted this kind of reasoning. I could see her temper ignite, like the soft blue flame of a pilot light. But I also detected that wonderful thing about her in that, till this day, she refuses to be combative, refuses to dispute a point, refuses in fact anything that brings abrasion to human relationships—especially our own. But beyond her household chores, my bride was especially adept at business matters. Using the skills she had learned as a professional secretary, she kept reports, day-by-day data and a myriad of other items which helped us organize the business.

Stopping at night became a feature of each day. I made sales stops during business hours, which altered the predictability of any particular place we might stop. Sometimes Juanita would find an appealing locale on the map, a lake or river or such, which offered potential. Invariably, however, the end of the day would occur many miles short of the locale or, on occasion, we might even drive past it. Also, as we drove, we would see ideal locations, some so attractive it became difficult not to stop early.

But we kept on our routine, mile after mile with towns and hamlets as stopovers. We found city parks attractive, also country schoolyards and an occasional abandoned farm. But the standard we had set on our first night—stopping at a filling station—became our foremost selection, although we would at times settle for an especially attractive park or waterway even though a service station facility might also be available.

As we traveled south, escaping the chill of winter, we came into many outdoor recreation areas. Juanita was a bit startled, and I suppose disappointed, to learn that I cared nothing about sports. Hunting and fishing were foreign words to me. She, on the other hand, had often accompanied her father and brother on outdoor sporting activities. She was a sports enthusiast herself, and was especially adept in swimming and diving.

We reached as far south as Corpus Christi, Texas, in our travels. Income was slim but steady. We made about a $2 markup on the sale of our silver collectors. I projected a first year income of $12,000, which proved to be accurate.

We took only living expenses out of the cash flow, no actual salary. Juanita used money unselfishly. She had saved from her working salary and added her own funds to the kitty as needed.

"You'll be on regular salary someday," I promised, as we sat in a scenic area we had chosen for the night's camp.

Moving her chair closer, she put her hand on mine and said, "We're in this thing together, remember." Taking her Bible, she opened it to the book of Ruth and read, "Wherever you go, I will go; and wherever you lodge, I will lodge. Your people shall be my people, and your God, my God" (Ruth 1:16. NKJV).

An old-fashioned romance like ours has its foundations firm in the counsels of the Bible!

Beginning a Family

We spent a year on the road with our trailer house, and enjoyed ourselves as we crisscrossed the central plains. We allowed ourselves a salary of $14 a week, stretching every penny to its farthest potential.

One day, when we had come full circle, I asked Juanita if she could spare an hour.

"Depends what for," she replied, gesturing to a large stack of clothes she was mending.

"I thought we'd look for a house," I said. I expected her to be off of her chair in a bounce, but instead, she sat quietly a moment and then reached and drew a sheet of paper toward her.

"I've been going over our accounts this morning," she said. "Our finances are certainly encouraging, but don't you think it's a little bit early to start looking for a house? Maybe we should wait a couple of months."

I looked at her in appreciation and amazement. What a perfect wife the Lord had given to me!

"I'd be able to live in this trailer for five years if necessary," she told me.

So we didn't mention the possibility again for several months. Then the day came when I felt it was time to begin house hunting. But again Juanita protested.

"Do you think we really should?" she asked softly. "Would it be wise to wait awhile yet?"

"Real estate is about the best equity a young couple can invest in," I said. "Besides, we can use a house as an initial base of operations."

It wasn't hard to convince her. We found a house which was nicer than we had imagined but still within our financial boundaries. During the initial years of our partnership, we had been able to save exactly the amount we needed for a cash purchase.

"Let's see this as from God's hand," I said. Tears came to her eyes. She nodded.

Slowly but assuredly, our little Tamco operations continued to grow. Our twosome family took on added dimensions too with the birth of our first child just two and a half years after our marriage.

I sat in a chair at the hospital trying to sleep when a nurse came to me in high excitement to exclaim, "Congratulations, Mr. Tam! You have a baby boy!"

I rushed to Juanita's side just in time to hear the doctor say to the two of us, "Congratulations on your new baby girl!"

"May I name her?" I asked my wife.

"What would your choice be?" she wanted to know.

"Rachel," I replied.

"Rachel," she echoed the word. "It's beautiful and fits her well."

We both looked at our lovely little daughter for a long and silent moment, convinced that on June 26, 1941, the prettiest baby ever born at Lima Memorial Hospital had made her appearance, despite the fact that the nurse had said she was a boy.

Juanita remained in the hospital for ten days. We still have the receipts for the charges we paid—$50 to the hospital, the same amount to the doctor.

Before her fifth birthday, Rachel opened her heart to the Lord Jesus. She lived a vital Christian life through high school, then went on to Nyack College. She met and married Jack Williams, a partner in a civil engineering firm. Their two children are Heather and Brian.

When our daughters were little girls, Juanita prayed that each of them would find a Christian husband. God answered that prayer, Jack among them. He became a cherished son-in-law, thus increasing our shock when, at age fifty-five, the Lord took him from us with a sudden heart attack. A fine businessman, father and husband, Jack had wisely and carefully looked after the physical needs of his wife and children should such an unanticipated event occur.

Our second child, Rebecca was born December 16, 1944, and, like her older sister, opened her heart to the Lord before her fifth birthday. She attended Houghton College where one day I picked her up for the Christmas holidays.

She told me there were three fellows that would like rides back as far as Lima. One of them especially caught my attention and, when we reached home, I told Becky she ought to keep an eye on that young man. She did. Today Wesley Lytle is the father of their two girls, Jennifer and Kristin, and has succeeded me as President and CEO of our three companies.

Five years to the day of Rachel's birth, Prudence joined our family. She also accepted Christ before she was five, lived a strong Christian life all through high school and on to Asbury College where she met Darrell Long. Dr. Long, I should say, because he is a surgeon. They have three children, Stuart, Sarah and Stanley.

Our fourth and last child was Candace—Candy, as we lovingly called her—born July 24, 1950.

When I asked her if she wanted to do as her sisters had done she sweetly replied, "I already asked Jesus into my heart during Vacation Bible School." She was under five at the time. Like her sisters, she was a consistent Christian all through high school, on to John Brown University for one year, then transferred to Olivet Nazarene College to study home economics. She met Paul VonTobel, who is in the lumber business. They also have three children, Michelle, Paul and Peter.

Highlights of my story are detailed in other parts of this book. For now, I would like to give you excerpts of a letter from our daughter Prudy in which she gives some insights which are very precious to me. She writes:

> Growing up at 800 South Pears Boulevard was a happy time for me. My mother was a homemaker; capable of doing most anything, from sewing dresses to planning and overseeing the construction of an addition to our house while Dad was overseas.
>
> She sang solos, did beautiful painting on china, yet could wield a hammer or screwdriver with the skill of a man.
>
> Although my dad was often gone on work and ministry assignments, he was by no means an absentee father in our home. One of my early memories is of the first time my dad came home at night and, wrapping me in his gray wool coat, he placed me under the piano bench until I could guess where I was. His coat smelled like the silver factory, and I liked that.

Whenever I became ill and missed a day of school, Dad would come home from work and go up right away to my room to pray with me. I really liked that because I felt so isolated upstairs with all the hubbub going on downstairs. I continue to have much confidence in my Dad's prayers and the God to whom he prays.

Do's and don'ts were very well defined in our home and we always knew when our big toe crossed over the line. Mine did frequently, because I always had to have the last word. I probably received the most spankings of the four girls. My mom would often write infractions on a piece of paper during the day, and my dad would then take disciplinary action when he arrived home at night. Discipline was simple and effective.

He would go down in the basement, sit on a certain chair and count one, two, three. Whichever number we arrived on was how many spankings we received. I never remember him spanking me in anger. He always told us how much he loved us. If the infraction occurred at church, we were taken to the basement, disciplined and taken back to the same pew from which we had come. Embarrassing? Yes.

There is, however, great security in knowing your parameters. Also, after being disciplined, somehow you felt clean, as if you had paid for your infractions and could go on with a clean slate—a very practical example of what God does for us when we are repentant and ask Him to forgive our sins. He also frees us from guilt.

Dad was a good storyteller. Our favorite had us falling through a hole in the ground and finding ourselves in Candy Land, where drinking fountains had soda pop in them and tree trunks were made of chocolate and whatever a child's heart could have longed for suddenly appeared. I remember coming home from school and finding Mom ironing dresses, shirts, aprons, handkerchiefs and the like while she listened to a radio drama. She would always quickly put her work aside to fix some nice snack for us girls. Grandma Lindeman took over that task whenever she happened to be visiting from Rockford. She would warm Swedish Rye bread and cut it into diamond shapes.

As time passed, we girls realized the business was doing very well. I remember asking my dad, "Are we rich?" To this he would always reply, "We are rich toward God."

He always got up very early to read his Bible and pray. Sometimes, when I came downstairs a bit early, I would find him praying aloud, and I would stand enthralled to hear him pray for each of us, our futures, the business mission, missionaries, on and on and on.

"Prayerlessness is a tool of Satan," he would tell us.

At 7:30 every morning, we would have family devotions. We read from the Bible, Danny Orlis books and the like. Dad always read the Bible. Mom read the storybooks, then we would pray together.

We had many missionaries for whom we prayed by name. We also kept a missionary bulletin board, by which we became familiar with missionaries overseas. Many of these people came into my own private prayers, apart from family devotions. Sometimes, when we were having our morning prayer time, neighbor kids would join us if they arrived a bit early to ride with us to school.

Our family life verse was Matthew 6:33, "Seek ye first the kingdom of God, and his righteousness; and all these things shall be added unto you" (KJV).

We girls looked on sadly as neighbor after neighbor installed television sets. Our father had not made a specific pronouncement but his silence spoke eloquently to the fact that, as far as he was concerned, he would never introduce one of those worldly boxes into our house. We girls began to break the silence, asking when we might expect to secure a television set. On a plea for family democracy, we asked if we might vote on whether to purchase this disputed item in our home.

Craftily our dad suggested we vote between a television or an organ. We voted—five votes for television, one for the organ. We realized that Mom had joined our forces even though we knew how much she wanted an organ. Even so, Dad announced that, all things considered, he'd decided that we would get the organ. Most of us took organ lessons and kept silent for a long time about television.

Sunday mornings, as we drove to church, we always listened to the Dr. DeHahn's Radio Bible Class. We never missed a Sunday morning in church, nor Sunday evening, nor midweek Bible study.

Even when we traveled away from home on the weekend our parents always found a place for us to worship on Sunday. We had four pastors at our church while we girls were growing up. I never heard my parents speak one word of criticism against any of them.

Christmas was a gala time at our house. Quite in contrast to what you might expect, one Christmas we allowed Santa himself to enter our home. We girls got really excited, trying not to give in to the suspicion that it was Grandpa Lindeman playing the part. Then the Christmas after his death, Grandma tried to fill the role. But when Santa's trousers fell down, the spell was broken.

In spite of the Santa intrusion, there was never any question in my mind about Jesus being real, Santa make-believe, and those lovely gifts we opened Christmas Eve came from parents and other loved ones.

The reality of Jesus, of course, was emphasized by the way our parents lived, the very objectives they had in life. We talked to Him in our prayers. We read about Him in the Bible. Also, our mother and father wanted us to know Jesus personally. It wasn't the same with Santa. When they talked about him it was always with a wink of the eye.

As teenagers, both Becky and Prudy became keenly interested in missions. They received an invitation from the Oriental Missionary Society to visit the mission in Medellin, Colombia.

Money remained quite tight for us those days, but Juanita and I decided we must let them go, realizing how valuable the experience would be for them. Right on time, knowing how the Lord does things, an uncle I scarcely knew left me an inheritance of $600, exactly the amount needed for the air tickets.

Becky and Prudy would be traveling alone, so in order for them to change planes only once, we bought their plane tickets out of Cincinnati. They would then meet a missionary lady in Miami, who would go on the same plane to Medellin.

Candy had heard about the Cincinnati Zoo, so the day we were to take the two girls to the airport, I promised that we would do our best to work the zoo into the schedule. Candy kept her eyes on her watch and the miles traveled, becoming disappointed as we approached Cincinnati too late to get to the zoo and also make the plane connection.

"We'll make a special trip to Cincinnati, someday," I said, trying to comfort her.

However, the plane Prudy and Becky were to take had mechanical problems, so they delayed the flight and listed it to leave in three hours. We jumped into the car, drove twenty-five miles back to the Cincinnati Zoo, which we went through at record speed. Candy was satisfied, in fact delighted, at the adventure of going so quickly through the facility.

We wouldn't have needed to hurry back to the airport, because it was several hours more until the flight finally took off. We had kept in touch with the missionary in Miami who was waiting at the gate when our daughters arrived. The two made the connection to Medellin in good order.

The missionaries took our two daughters into their hearts and gave them the time of their lives. They went down into the jungle and stayed in primitive houses. Boldly they ate the strange food, drank the boiled water, got acquainted with the nationals and spent two months in the "regions beyond."

When it came time for their return, we tried to arrange for someone to meet them and help them through Miami Airport. We could find no one. To the delight of Rachel and Candy, their mother and father decided to go all the way down to Miami and meet the returning girls. On the way, we stopped at Sea World. Excitement was marred when I picked up a newspaper and read that a plane coming in from Colombia had been hijacked. Our hearts sank. There were so few details, only a bulletin, but we couldn't help wondering if our two girls might be on that plane.

We did a lot of praying on our way to the Miami Airport.

It was a glorious moment when we saw Prudy and Becky come smiling off the plane to meet us.

In her letter, our daughter had also listed some truths she had been taught by her parents:

1. Keep your eyes on Jesus. Man will usually disappoint you, but Jesus never will.
2. God's Word is truth.
3. You advance by your reverses.
4. All we have is from God. We are stewards of our time, talent and money.

Yes, we had wonderful rapport as a family. I tried to be the best father I knew how to be. Most importantly, I tried to be a Christian father. I may have been overly strict at times but I'd rather have it that way than to be too permissive as is the case with many Christians today who are permissive to the point where they do serious damage to their children's spiritual development.

Prudy mentioned my wrapping her in my coat. I did this with all the children. Each of them would stand and wait while I took them, one at a time, wrapped up in my overcoat to some part of the house where I then held them in darkness until they guessed where they were. They loved that routine.

I can't ever remember wishing the girls were boys. They were such lovely young ladies. I did try to rough them up a bit, however, to keep them from being too dainty. I taught them tricks. I stood on my head and coached them until each of them could do the same. It was a startling moment for Juanita that day when she came upon us, father and four daughters standing on their heads in a row.

I tried not to get too rough. One night, however, tossing Becky around, she was screaming with delight and I did become a bit over-zealous, so much so that I dislocated her shoulder.

How sad that family life has deteriorated in so many instances these days. Sitting in front of a television set keeps the family together and yet, at the same time, it separates them. I thank God for the unity and togetherness we had as a growing family!

CHAPTER

EIGHTEEN

Business Unusual

Our Tamco Silver Collectors provided the foundation for our business. We became the first to succeed with precious metal reclamation. We should have been the fifth to go bankrupt, but along that roadside north of Columbus, Ohio, God had promised to make our business succeed and so failure was out of the question. Interestingly, the silver business gave rise to what has become the primary thrust of our operations. Now we mail out the new collectors and photo dealers send their silver-laden Tamcos back to us.

Back in the days when we still made "house calls," I noted the inferior quality of so many of the photo processing tanks. This led us into the development of the much superior plastic tanks and, consequently, the U.S. Plastics division of our company.

Plastics became the product base that provided our phenomenal economic growth, relegating Tamco Silver Collectors to a minor but continued item. We realized we couldn't major on the marketing of plastics and keep up on our never-ending tours out to pick up and replace collectors in photo studios, which involved hundreds of miles of driving and many days of time.

"Couldn't we try collecting by mail?" Juanita suggested one day, "We could send out replacements by mail as well."

"Do you think photographers would respond?" I questioned.

"It's worth a try," she said.

I was highly skeptical but, to my amazement, the silver collectors began to come in and we would mail new units to replace them. We also began doing mail promotion of plastic goods, with encouraging results.

Early one morning, as I sat with my Bible, I came to the eighth chapter of Deuteronomy where God reminded Moses that not only was he the conveyor of commandments to the people but, as their leader, was expected to make sure all commandments were obeyed—especially the eleventh verse, which reads, "Beware that thou forget not the LORD thy God, in not keeping his commandments, and his judgments, and his statutes, which I command thee this day" (KJV).

I grew tense, remembering the commitments I had made to the Lord concerning the business. A sense of expectancy came upon me as I realized the Lord seemed to have something special for me that day. At other times I have had similar experiences with the Scriptures, finding high adventure in the discovery of guidelines by which to lead my life and administer procedures. Such was very much the case this day as I read about God reminding Moses how He had led him through the wilderness and provided for him and the people so miraculously.

"Lord," I prayed that day, "I thank You again for Your sovereignty. Be totally Lord in my life, in control of everything—my thoughts, my decisions, my actions, everything."

Then, to my amazement, as I continued reading the eighth chapter of Deuteronomy, I found these words in the eighteenth verse: "Remember the LORD thy God: for it is he that giveth thee power to get wealth" (KJV). I realized that was God's statement as to the amazing capability of the Jewish people to prosper financially, but I also believe the Holy Spirit led me to that verse that morning. Then in the way He personalizes the Bible to us, Deuteronomy 8:18 became a promise for me to claim.

Now, I do not advocate opening your Bible and putting your finger down in the hopes that it will answer some need or question you have. But I have had some amazing experiences where the Lord has led me in a similar manner as this and has thereby guided me. The key, in my opinion, is to be sure you are led by the Holy Spirit to open the Bible and look for wisdom from the Lord. I believe the Lord can guide me anytime He wants to from any source in His word, and I rely on that, practice it and praise God for it.

You may have heard the bit of humor about the man who, confused with life, sought guidance. Opening his Bible at random, he put down his finger on Matthew 27:5, where Judas went and hanged himself. Upon closing and reopening his Bible, he again placed a finger by happenstance on Luke 10:37, where Jesus concluded the story of the Good Samaritan, saying, "Go, and do thou likewise" (KJV). Frustrated, he tried a third attempt. This time he put his finger on John 13:27, where Jesus told His betrayer, "What you do, do quickly" (NKJV). Obviously, this is no laughing matter. That is why I urge you to carefully seek and follow the guidance of the Holy Spirit when you search the Scriptures seeking directions from the Lord.

Both Juanita and I have had wonderful experiences using a seeking method of Scripture reading. Juanita had an amazing experience with Psalm 41:12. Let me say something here. When you actively and sincerely seek to live under the Lordship of Jesus Christ and the guidance of the Holy Spirit, I believe God can take any portion of Scripture He wishes and, the Holy Spirit having guided you to it, use that promise or precept for you to better understand His plan and purpose for you.

As I stated, despite the fact that plastics quickly surpassed silver collectors in providing our cash flow as a company, we continued to manufacture the silver collectors. Four times the silver business caused me to make course corrections in my effort to be solidly Christian in all aspects of our business.

The first of these involved Mr. Aukerman, the man in Cleveland, Ohio, from whom I had obtained rights to develop the Tamco Silver Collector. I discovered his patent was faulty and decided to consult a patent attorney who, after a thorough review of the situation, told me, "Mr. Aukerman's patent cannot be defended in court. I advise you to pay no more royalties. I will notify the inventor that he cannot hold you to the contract."

I told my wife about the situation. I could see it troubled her. "Is this maybe a situation where you go the second mile?" she asked.

To which I replied, hedging just a little, "It is a situation where it would be poor business procedure to assume a financial obligation where there is no legal constraint to do so."

My attorney notified Mr. Aukerman's attorney, with the result that the inventor reacted with vigorous protest. He sent his attorney to see me. "We think you should continue paying the royalties," the attorney said.

"But the patent is invalid," I argued.

"You have the reputation of a man of high integrity," the attorney countered. "Paying royalties is a matter of good faith."

"If the patent were valid," I said, "I wouldn't hesitate for a moment. But you know yourself that if you took the matter to court, you would lose. I will stand on my rights as a citizen."

That ended the matter. Or so I thought. Three years passed. Our business continued to grow. I was named prayer chairman for the Lima Jack Shuler Crusade, and I went from church to church on midweek nights to urge prayer for the coming outreach.

Let me be just a bit facetious. Let me give you a little advice on how to backslide. If you become involved in something which grieves the Holy Spirit, as my treatment of Mr. Aukerman certainly did, stay as far away from prayer meetings as you possibly can. For prayer, you see, gives the Holy Spirit the climate and terrain He needs to speak to your deepest heart. He surely spoke to mine.

One evening, as I was addressing a prayer group in a Lima church, I said, "You know, folks, we don't need to wait until the revival begins to have one in our own hearts. We can have that right now."

Zing! Like an arrow, my own words came back to strike me full force, setting my conscience afire. It troubled me so I couldn't sleep that night, and I remained restless and confused the next day. I paced the floor of our home long after we had finished dinner.

My wife brought me a cup of coffee. "Something troubling you?" she asked.

So I told her. "I'm going to go see Mr. Aukerman," I said.

"The sooner the better," she replied.

"It's the business of obedience," I told Juanita, my closest confidant—and dearest friend. "I want to obey God in everything."

"Obey the Lord, Stanley," she urged quietly. "Go the extra mile. It will be worth it." I did meet Mr. Aukerman, and spent several hours with him and his daughter and their attorney. They suggested a cash settlement which would not involve any more royalties. The amount they requested was within $500 of what I thought would be a fair arrangement, so I signed the papers that same day.

In the following December, the aging inventor suffered a massive stroke and died. Unfortunately, I don't know Mr. Aukerman's status with his Maker, but I do know that great peace came to my own heart as I thanked the Lord for guiding me to making things right with Mr. Aukerman before he passed away. What I also know, with great joy, is that because of my obedience to the Lord, Mr. Aukerman's daughter opened her heart to Christ!

Let me share something with you, friend. Whenever you obey God by putting things right with another person whom you have wronged, the blessing you receive can linger through the years—enriching your thoughts, your prayer life, even adding to the impact of the Bible as you read it. Also, you receive a special inner growth whereby you are prepared to face ensuing circumstances with a maturity you did not possess in the early years of your Christian experience. Obedience is the key to spiritual wholeness and vitality. I like the way The Living Bible puts it in Psalm 51:12, "Make me willing to obey you."

You see, obedience doesn't come to us naturally. Obedience comes to us supernaturally! In Psalm 100:1-2 of The Living Bible, we are told to "Shout with joy before the Lord, O earth! Obey him gladly."

In my book *God's Woodshed*, you will find numerous examples of how God rewards obedience with spiritual enrichment. Let me share two or three examples with you here.

In 1956, a company in Washington, D.C. developed the first electric silver reclaimer. When I saw it demonstrated at a photographic convention, my mind went on a rampage. I knew this was exactly what we needed. The electric unit was far superior to the galvanic type we had obtained some twenty years earlier.

"It's the difference between a Model T or a V8," I told Juanita. "Those electric collectors collect four times faster than the units we're now using."

"Did you do any negotiations with those people?" my wife asked.

"We need to develop a unit of our own," I replied. She looked at me with those probing eyes that had become so important to me through our many years together, but she didn't say anything.

First, we began a research department, adding a full-time chemical engineer. We wanted our collector to be different from anything else, and we also wanted it to be better. I began looking for a patent firm. We considered ourselves fortunate to find a group of patent attorneys in nearby Dayton, Ohio. In eighteen months, we had our own set of blueprints. "You're clean as a whistle, Mr. Tam," the Dayton patent attorneys assured me.

"Oh, Lord," I prayed, "this is Your silver collector, not mine. Bless it. Protect it. Use it to produce large sums of money with which to do Your work." My heart surged with peace and joy!

When I put our prototype to the test, it performed perfectly. Thrilling!

"I planned to feature it at the next photo finisher's convention," I told Juanita.

"Sounds exciting," she replied, but then realized that I had said I had *planned* to feature it at the photo finisher's convention.

"You aren't going to exhibit it?" she asked.

"There's just one little problem," I added.

""What's that?"

"The next convention is in Washington D.C."

"So?"

"That's where the company is located that made the first electrical collector, the one that got me so excited I had no choice but to create our own."

"What does that matter?" my wife asked. She is so astute in so many ways. "If you made a new model, cleared by patent attorneys, you're OK, aren't you?"

"Sure," I agreed. "But I'd actually be a lot more comfortable out in some place like San Francisco or maybe down in Dallas."

"I can't see what it matters where you show it," Juanita said, "since you have the patents registered and approved."

So, with some trepidation, I set up our display booth at the convention in Washington, and drew an immediate crowd. To my consternation, one of those who came to see our unit was none other than the original inventor himself, the man who owned the company in Washington from which we had received the first inspiration to develop our own silver collector. He went into an immediate uproar!

"You're a thief!" he shouted. "You're infringing on my silver collector. I'll have you in court immediately!"

I went up to my room at the hotel and, falling to my knees beside the bed, began to pray. "What did I do wrong this time?" I whined to the Lord. "Don't those patent attorneys know what they're doing? Have they taken me to the cleaners?"

I didn't sleep much that night, but the next morning I somehow mustered the courage to get back to my booth. Several people had heard the outburst of the inventor, and the story spread across the convention floor. I packed up early and headed back home.

Juanita was wonderful. She didn't give me any "I told you so" treatment.

I promptly received a court summons, just as the man in Washington had threatened. Somewhat frightened, and bitterly disappointed, I headed down to Dayton and showed the summons to the attorney.

"What's wrong?" I asked. "Didn't you guys provide me with good patents?"

"You have good patents," the leader of the group said in a civil manner as compared to my disturbed attitude.

"I'm sorry," I said, settling down as soon as I could. "It's just that—"

"It's somewhat like trying to get a patent for a toothbrush," the man continued. "The engineering is so elementary, there isn't much to add to make it completely distinctive from the original. There isn't much innovation you can give to one of these silver collectors. But yours is definitely different." It sounded like some hastily concocted legalese to me. I wanted to ask these men why they hadn't told me these things in the first place, rather than say I had a clean patent.

"You can defend it in court?" I asked testily.

"The margins of distinctions are very close," the man said. I felt sure he was being evasive.

"Your best procedure would be to entertain a contractual agreement with the actual inventor, so you can buy his product and pass it on to your customers."

My spirits plummeted. I had another one of those tortuous ninety-minute drives back to Lima, and I wrestled with God every mile.

"Is this par for the course," I asked, "when a man tries to please You? I'll eat crow if I must, but doesn't that demean Your name, Lord? This guy knows I made You my senior partner."

"What will you do?" Juanita asked when I got home and told her what the lawyers had said.

"I don't have any other choice," I replied.

"So you're going to see if you can buy the collectors out of Washington instead of trying to manufacture them here in Lima?"

I nodded.

Business appointments in Chicago came up. I completed my work in Chicago in the late afternoon and opted against the long drive back to Lima. I may as well have driven because I had a sleepless night. I arose early the next morning to have my devotions. My hotel room seemed more like a prison cell.

In my devotional routines, I have a plan whereby I read through the Bible once every year. At that time I was back to the Old Testament, making my way laboriously through the genealogies of David's descendants. Barely able to keep my mind from wandering, I half-closed my Bible as I sat for several moments in a state of nagging discouragement.

Abruptly, a Scripture I had read several days earlier came to mind, standing out like an engraving. I turned back to the second chapter of Judges to the record of where Joshua was leading the people into the land of Canaan. There in the second verse of the second chapter, I read the Lord's counsel to the great leader: "You shall make no covenant with the inhabitants of this land" (NKJV). This divine dictum, delivered by Joshua to the people he was leading, came to my mind as clearly as though a voice had spoken it to me. The Lord impressed upon my mind and heart that He did not want me to enter into any contract with the Washington D.C. firm.

Upon returning home the next day, I immediately made an appointment with the patent office in Dayton. "I value your counsel," I said, hedging a bit. "Obviously, you are much more knowledgeable in this matter than I am. It was my full intent to follow your advice but I simply cannot enter into an arrangement of any kind with this Washington inventor. I want to go through with the court appointment and I want you to represent me."

A look of stark dismay came to the faces of those men. They huddled a few moments, then the spokesman for the group said, "We can't represent you, Mr.Tam."

"Under no circumstances," said one of the others.

"As I told you before," continued the spokeman, "we believe the margins are very tight. You could very possibly lose, and have this man sue you for everything you own. You could lose your business, your home, your savings—everything."

Were my ears deceiving me? Weren't these the men who had given me such bright assurances? Could they possibly be shysters, manipulating me for the dollars I was willing to spend?

I tried to press the matter further, but made no headway. That drive home was, more than ever, a time of deep introspection and discouragement. I tried to pray, but it was useless. Words fell unspoken upon my tongue. I began thinking about the possibilities, worrying up a storm of anxiety for myself. Were the attorneys, whatever their motives, telling the truth when they said I could lose everything?

Should I jump the gun? See if I can file for bankruptcy? The Lord rebuked me.

More like rigamarole than intercession, I continued pouring out my misgivings to my Lord. At last, in desperation, I cried out, "Well OK, God! I give up! I'll face that court alone, trusting completely in You!" You never know Christ until Christ is all that you have.

Once again, Juanita was wonderful. She agreed with my decision and promised to stand by me in prayer. Prayer had become uniquely meaningful to her at that time. She had begun a procedure whereby she wove promises from the Bible into the text of her prayers. Take, for example, Psalm 23. Realizing the scope of my perplexities, she would likely pray, "Lord, You clearly tell us in the Bible that You are our Shepherd. Please be with dear Stanley. Be his Shepherd. Teach him anew how to be one of Your lambs. And You also say, I shall not want. Well, Lord, my husband wants peace and a sure sense of guidance. That promise in Philippians 4:19, is like Psalm 23, isn't it, Lord? 'My God shall supply all your need according to His riches in glory by Christ Jesus' (NKJV)."

The Lord answered my wife's prayer. He also answered mine. I can't explain how we got out of the problem, except for the all things that stand behind a Christian when he really puts God's promises on the line.

First, my not going to the court hearing on the date it had been scheduled was no trivial matter, my excuse being that I had received no official reminder.

Second, great peace had come to my mind and heart. I awakened every morning with this peace and carried it with me through the day. When I awakened in the morning, I had peace. When I went into my office, I felt peace. When I moved around the plant, observing operations, peace. In everything I had peace. It was fantastic! The end of the story is simply that I never did hear from the court. I received no word of any kind from anyone in Washington.

Then came the clincher. I heard a news report about a bizarre accident involving the inventor who had filed the suit against me. It seems he was working alone in his plant late one night. He went in and out of a secure vault where he kept his silver. The vault had an iron door. All I know is what I read in the paper.

The following morning, the man's employees found him. Somehow, the iron door to his vault had come loose, falling on him and knocking him down and pinning him. He could not free himself. He was dead. That was the last I ever heard. I know nothing about that man's soul. I don't know why he did not press the court appointment. With all my heart, I wish he could have lived, no matter what the cost would have been to me, so that perhaps I would have had a chance to talk to him about his need for salvation.

It was another of my incredible adventures with God. "In his heart a man plans his course, but the LORD determines his steps" (Proverbs 16:9).

After that first year when we so successfully tested the use of the mail as a substitute to barnstorming the Midwest, our business grew. Slowly at first, like a rocket after countdown, we experienced an upsurge in business marketing volume. With the surging momentum, we did $16,000 gross the second year. Then $45,000, then $90,000, $150,000, multiplying year after year into the millions.

Then I made a staggering discovery that would become the third test of my integrity as a Christian involving our silver collectors. For ten years, I had been smelting the silver into a purified liquid, pouring the liquid into molds which, when the liquid cooled, formed the semi-precious metal into solid bars, which I sold to a firm in Chicago.

The thought occurred to me that it might be a better procedure to have a second source for selling the silver. Shortly, I learned of a refinery in Connecticut, wrote to them and received a prompt reply that they would be happy to purchase any amount of silver I could provide.

Exuberant and optimistic, I sent a substantial shipment, anticipating a check as was always the case with my Chicago outlet.

Instead, I received a stern note from the refinery CEO, informing me that I had neglected to enclose the Internal Revenue Stamps required by the government for the sale of silver in any amount. I was dumbfounded. I had never heard of such government stamps and wrote asking for information. The buyer seemed as astonished as I was dumbfounded. He included a booklet of tax information. Browsing the booklet, I saw I needed a license to sell silver. Further, I learned that, without a license, I must pay the government twenty percent commission on every sale and that the amount would be retroactive!

In those moments of initial panic, a terrifying thought crossed my mind. I had been spared the wrath of the Washington D.C. inventor. Could it be, however, that now I would be bankrupted by the government itself?

My mind began to work as I realized the implications of this new knowledge. Could I somehow shunt aside the facts that glared at me that day, sweep under the rug of ignorance the thousands of dollars I would not be able to pay in taxes? Could I begin from scratch, applying for a license as though I were just getting into the silver business?

Well, let me tell you something. Whenever you decide to be deceitful, stay away from the Bible! Otherwise, like I did, you're likely to run into such verses as Galatians 6:7: "Do not be deceived, God is not mocked; for whatever a man sows, that he will also reap" (NKJV). Be advised. God also has plan two. God's message to me through His Word was, on this occasion, found in the chapter immediately following Psalm 23: "Who may ascend into the hill of the LORD? Or who may stand in His holy place? He who has clean hands and a pure heart" (Psalm 24:3-4, NKJV).

"Lord," I cried out, "I don't want to have anything that isn't pleasing in Your sight. I'm going to bite the bullet." I did exactly that.

Bringing in the statistics out of our business from its beginning, I went to the Lima office of the IRS and explained the problem. They, in turn, sent me to the district office in Toledo, where I was referred to the Miscellaneous Tax Division, where I again explained my plight. They began searching through their books and found the law on silver.

"It says here," a lady told me, "you must have a license before you can sell any silver. We will refer your information to Washington."

With the information I had gotten by that time, I figured I owed the government just under $25,000—an astronomical sum at that point in the history of our fledgling organization!

That night, after Juanita had gone to bed, I turned off the lights, got down on my knees and cried out to the Lord. "Why are you putting me through this situation, Lord?" I complained. "Haven't I been fair enough with You? You know I have made You part owner of the business, how I faithfully pay the thousands of dollars we promised for overseas ministry. OK, go ahead and close me out. Bankrupt me. Let me find a job in a factory someplace where I can work eight hours and go home and not fear any problems."

Have you ever complained like that? We have a patient God, don't we? In my case, the Lord waited until I got all of my complaints off my chest. Then He spoke to me.

"Stanley," His voice remains clear in my memory, "the problem isn't in your business. The problem is in your heart. You have sin in your heart, Stanley. You know what is the greatest sin in the world?" I heard the Lord ask. "Is it murder? Adultery? No, I'll tell you what it is. It's unbelief! Just now, as you are praying to Me, you don't really believe I can answer your prayers. But listen, Stanley. If you will take care of this sin of unbelief in your heart, I'll take care of the problem in your business."

That night, as nearly as I could determine the Holy Spirit's leading, I obeyed the Lord and tried my utmost to face myself honestly. I listened to God's voice like a child being reproved by his parent. With penitent tears, I opened my Bible and began thumbing through the pages. I came to the thirty-second chapter of Jeremiah, where the twenty-seventh verse leaped out at me like a neon sign: "Behold, I am the LORD, the God of all flesh. Is there anything too hard for me?" (NKJV).

Nothing is too hard for my omnipotent God! A breath of peace came to my heart, the promise of assurance to my mind. I remained tense, apprehensive, but no longer in despair. I dared to believe God would undertake for me!

Then I found First Peter 5:7: "Casting all your care upon Him, for He cares for you" (NKJV). Peace came fully to my heart, assurance to my mind—the peace and assurance we can have when, by obedient faith, we try to cast all our cares upon the Lord. The peace and assurance that comes is a result of faith in its highest function.

Silver refining itself gave me the illustration I needed for those trying days. We receive the silver collectors in raw form. We put the accumulated silver into a furnace, which we heat to smelting intensity. The furnace not only liquefies the raw metal, it purifies it as well. So it is with the Lord and His children. He promises in Isaiah 1:25, "I will . . . thoroughly purge away your dross, and take away all your alloy" (NKJV).

It was painful at first, but what a blessing to be made pure—purified so I could serve Him better!

Well, you might say that all this sounds like good Christian psychology, but does it pay the bills? I want to tell you how that bill got paid. How—once again—I experience another incredible adventure with God.

With my renewed trust in the Lord, having cast all cares upon my senior partner, the Lord Himself took over. He made repeated trips to the IRS headquarters in Washington. He knew exactly which staff member's heart could be touched on my behalf. After one year, the IRS issued its ruling.

Convinced of my innocence and good will, they forgave the unpaid taxes. Instead, they issued a penalty against me of $467. I could proceed from that point as if I were a newcomer just getting started. Hallelujah!

"Dishonest money dwindles away, but he who gathers money little by little makes it grow" (Proverbs 13:11).

Always remember that, whereas God often offers to work with us, His preferred process is to work through us. He inspires our minds, guides our hands and directs our feet. His promise in Psalm 32:8 is, "I will instruct you and teach you in the way you should go; I will guide you with My eye" (NKJV). He instructs us and guides us, but the doing and going is left to us. The requisite for this instruction and guidance is always to be clean and obedient. When you seek to follow the Christlike life, you can expect God to check up on you to test your motivations.

For example, at one time we made a shipment of silver to a refiner in Chicago expecting a check in the amount of $2,000. Instead we received a check for $5,000, and believe me, it was at a time when we could have used that extra $3,000. Was I tempted to keep the money? Of course I was. But I had a commitment with God—not just a partial commitment and not just when I was in a jam and needed help—but a commitment involving every transaction, every moment of every day.

I wrote a brief note to the Chicago firm suggesting they do a new assay. They, thinking I was displeased with the amount, agreed and were amazed to find the $3,000 error. I received a two-page letter of gratitude. By mistake, the assay numbers had been interchanged and there would have been no way of tracing it without my letter.

A short time later on a trip to Chicago, Mr. Goldsmith, vice president of the firm, invited me to lunch with himself and four other key members of his staff.

"Mr. Tam," Goldsmith asked as we sat eating, "what do you mean when you say God is your senior partner?"

"It's a long story," I said.

Without so much as glancing at his watch he said, "We'll take the time."

For the next hour it was my privilege to tell those men the miracle God had brought in my life, the redemption of my soul and the guidance for my activities. I didn't detect the slightest skepticism in the eyes of those men. When you refund a man $3,000, he believes you when you tell him why you did it.

* * *

When I read through my Bible every year, I always enjoy Old Testament history. I was reading through the fifteenth chapter of First Samuel and came upon this verse: "To obey is better than sacrifice, and to heed than the fat of rams" (1 Samuel 15:22, NKJV). The Bible is full of little gems such as that verse. You can be reading along someplace and then, in a burst of glory, such a statement appears. This is one of my favorites: "To obey is better than sacrifice, and to heed than the fat of rams."

Let me share the experience of how this Scripture enriched my life during one of my adventures with God.

When we closed our books one year, our bookkeeper came to my office and said, "I'm sorry to tell you about a small matter, Mr. Tam, but knowing how careful you are, even in the small details, I felt I should do it." Then he showed me how, through the year, we had sold more silver than they had figured into the commissions we paid to our customers. "We owe about $4,000 to 3,000 customers," our bookkeeper said. "As I say, it's a small matter, and can easily be written off."

"Any special reason for the slipup?" I asked.

"We probably ran the assays too low," he replied. "Like, say, the silver was ninety-five percent pure, and we called it ninety-four and three quarters percent, giving us the overage. In most instances, it only amounted to pennies, others a few dollars. We could send back the higher amounts, forget the others, couldn't we?" I thanked him and he went back to his room. I didn't give the matter much thought, because I was in a hurry to clear off my work so we could be on our way in less than a week to Rockford for the Christmas holiday.

A couple of days later, however, as I was praying, the thought came to me that, since we were in the concluding days of December, I should be thinking about taking inventory. So I prayed, "God, is there anything in my life that is not pleasing to You?"

I've learned through the years that this kind of prayer invariably sets things into motion. Even so, it startled me just a bit to have God remind me of the $4,000.

"Lord," I said, "we have 3,000 customers."

"But," the Lord laid on my heart, "you still have $4,000 that doesn't belong to you."

Have you ever noticed that the Lord is interested in small things? He tells us that if we will be faithful in little things He knows we will be faithful in big things, but, if we are unfaithful in the small things, He knows we will be unfaithful in the big things as well.

In other words, God tests us with small things to see if He can promote us to the big things. At that moment, on my knees, I knew I had two options: Obey God and let His power flow through me, or disobey Him.

How well I remembered times when I had disobeyed my Lord. It was like pulling a switch. The power of God left me and I was miserable until I made things right. I decided not to play any games. God was speaking to me about a little thing, and I was determined to obey Him.

Those days in Rockford with Juanita's family added up to the most joyful Christmas I could remember. The carols had a new ring to them. As we read the timeless story, it became warmly contemporary.

"Joy to the World," we sang. "Joy to Stanley Tam!" echoed in my heart!

As soon as I got back to Lima, I hired a new girl who spent six weeks going over our books to determine how much each customer was to receive. For some, the amount was so small we decided to pay them in postage stamps. But the point is we paid them—each one.

It was great fun, day-after-day, seeing the list grow. We had a lot of laughs.

Finally, 3,000 envelopes were ready to go into the mail. We didn't mail them, however, not right away, because again the Lord spoke to me with a suggestion that we enclose a letter in each envelope explaining why we were doing the refund. This, naturally, would include information about God being our senior partner with all profits going to Him.

"I doubt if we'll get any response," I told members of our staff, "because we mention God so prominently."

We weren't prepared for the results. Hundreds of letters came in the mail, as customers told us how glad they were that we had God as our senior partner. In fact we got a letter from a Catholic sister at a hospital in Logansport, Indiana, saying, "Thank you for the refund. We don't use your silver collectors for the money. We use them for the gospel tracks we find inside. We all read them."

I went down to our local camera shop to check on something relative to photographs we use in our catalog. The manager insisted on giving me back the money we had sent—a little over $3, or something like that—telling me also about salesmen who dropped by for the express purpose of asking about this Stanley Tam character.

I was told that "Nothing we have ever done in advertising has caught the attention of clients, or solicited new business, like the matter of simply doing the right thing."

One day I called on one of our older customers. At the sight of me, he lit up with sheer pleasure and said, "Am I glad to see you! As you know, our finishing department is over in another building nearby. Our plant manager, Bud Eaton, works over there. Every time he receives replacement collectors and finds those gospel tracts inside, he hits the roof. He cusses up a storm, and bellows about what kind of company do you have over there in Lima that pitches religion along with business. 'What's their angle?' That's the way he puts it.

"Then the day came when we got your refund check and that awesome letter. Seventeen bucks the check was, or something like that. I took the check down to show Bud.

"Bud said we hadn't sent any silver, so no money was due. Then I showed him the letter. It bowled him over. He read it through twice. Then he said, 'Well, if they are that honest because of their religion, or whatever, they were probably right to pitch those gospel tracts to us the way they do. As a matter of fact, I'm going to read the ones that come next time.'"

One day I received a letter from an Ed Haas in Stamford, Connecticut. He was formerly one of our customers, but had gone out of business, and was now on the road selling some non-photographic products.

"As I go driving around New England, representing my product," he wrote to me, "I drop in to see some of my old friends. They are all talking about those refund checks you sent back and about how honest you are and how you are partners with God.

"I had an old photographer friend in Waterbury. He demonstrated one of your silver collectors to me. Mr. Tam, I could sell those like popcorn at a ball game. Any chance I could add your collector to my line? I think I could drum up a lot of customers for you."

I knew next to nothing about this Ed Haas, but I decided to give him a try. So I sent him a few collectors and a page of instructions.

"See how well I'm doing?" he wrote after a couple of months. "Why don't you hire me full time?"

I asked him to come see me and he came right away. I felt some slight tension when he entered my office. After all, I didn't have much expertise in handling fireballs.

"It's pretty obvious by looking at me that I'm Jewish," he began. "Hope that's no problem."

"It's an enhancement, Mr. Haas," I said.

"An enhancement!" he exclaimed. "How can that be?"

"First of all, I have a very warm affinity toward Jewish people."

"That's interesting," he said. His eyes began to glow. "Usually it's the opposite. You got lots of Jewish friends?"

"You're the first," I told him.

Then he looked at me for a long, silent interim. He cocked his head first to one side and then the other. He grew sober, but, gradually, brought that winsome smile back to his face. "What is it you like about us so much?"

"It's what you've given us."

"What's that?"

I breathed a silent prayer, hesitated a moment, then said, "It's your race that gave us my Savior, the Lord Jesus Christ."

He stepped back, intense and serious. I wondered if I had offended him. "Yeah," he said. "Jesus was a Jew, wasn't He? I'm not much into religion." Ed Haas and Stanley Tam established a vital rapport in that moment!

It didn't take long to realize what a wise move it was hiring Ed full time. We kept in close touch. One afternoon, Ed called. "I've got more and more problems with a little situation," he began.

"What's that, Ed?" I asked.

"It's that religious literature you send to people," he said cautiously.

"You don't like that we do that?"

"I love it," he said. "I read every one of those little pamphlets. My problem is that so many times when people learn I'm from your place in Lima, they begin asking questions about the Bible and stuff. Would it be OK if I send those questions on to you?"

"Sure, Ed. I'll take care of every question as soon as I receive it."

"Boy, that's a relief," he said.

Then the glorious day came when I received a letter from Ed, saying, "I, too, am interested in your Jesus Christ." He came to Lima. We had him at our home for dinner. After the meal, my wife—wise in the tact of soul winning—took the kids upstairs. The two of us had only a brief talk. Ed was ready for salvation.

What a fantastic honor it was, kneeling beside a descendent of David and Abraham, and hearing him open his heart to his and my Messiah, the Lord Jesus.

Ed continued selling at his former pace. He was a phenomenon, really. He was also very brilliant. Tell him something once and he had it. It was especially true of the Bible. He got so he could handle the Bible like a seasoned instructor.

However, he only worked for us two years. Then I received a telephone call. Ed Haas had died of a heart attack. He had become a brother to me, in every sense of the word. I couldn't help remembering the reason—those refund checks! Oh, I could have kept those $4,000 and still remained a fairly acceptable Christian, but thank God, I didn't!

If I hadn't written that letter we inserted in the envelope with those refunds, many of our customers would never have learned about God being our senior partner. They could have easily thought somebody on our staff, somebody on our mailing room was slipping those tracts into the silver payments. There would be many people yet without Christ.

"To obey is better than sacrifice." The words ran though my thoughts like gentle thunder, like the whisper of an angel. But from somewhere in the past, I remembered the words: Our obedience determines the destiny of souls. Our disobedience does, also!

"Therefore if you have not been faithful in the use of unrighteous mammon, who will commit to your trust the true riches? And if you have not been faithful in what is another man's, who will give you what is your own? No servant can serve two masters; for either he will hate the one and love the other, or else he will be loyal to the one and despise the other. You cannot serve God and mammon" (Luke 16:11-13, NKJV).

CHAPTER

NINETEEN

Our World "Market"

We do not ship silver collectors to Jakarta and Caracas. Neither do we mail our plastics catalog to Seoul and Taipei. Yet we have an active "market" in each of those areas, plus many other overseas points. You see, we have commercial "markets" for our business but, far more important, we have spiritual markets involving outreach with the gospel to the souls of people overseas.

As I report to you in these moments, we are investing more than $3 million a year for evangelism in the regions beyond. I happen to believe that kind of "marketing"—reaching people with the gospel of Jesus Christ—is the most important business in all the world. I believe it is more important than selling computers, automobiles, aircraft, farm implements, food stuffs or medical provisions.

The company's foreign involvement dates back directly to that day when I pulled to a stop on the side of Highway 23 north of Columbus, Ohio, and heard God tell me that if I would turn my business over to Him, He would make it succeed. Previously, our involvement in missions had been typical of the run-of-the-pew church member. We gave through our church, had missionaries in our home, prayed daily for the harvest fields abroad. Only when we formed the Stanita Foundation and began directing company profits overseas did we become actively involved in missions. (See the Epilogue "Laying Up Treasures in Heaven" on page 162 for a documentation of my first trip around the world as a businessman steward for missions.)

I have made twenty-four crusade trips overseas. You might call them reconnaissance crusades, during which we did extensive surveys of the work underway, of places where we could improve and then also of areas not yet touched by our stewardship involvement.

The first such crusade trip was from late September until December 23, 1952. The ministry and survey took place in Hawaii, the Philippines, Taiwan, Japan, Korea, Thailand, India, Pakistan, Italy, France and England. Juanita did not accompany me on that first trek.

Over the next two years, I remained in North America, traveling extensively throughout the country to tell the story of what I saw God do in the harvest lands. Through the years, I have had well over 7,000 speaking engagements and have traveled a couple million miles by air and another million by car.

In January and February of 1955, we surveyed and ministered in Colombia, Ecuador, Peru and Brazil. Juanita was with me and, later in this chapter, I will relate how the Lord dealt with us as we traveled together.

In 1958, I spent two weeks in Puerto Rico with The Christian and Missionary Alliance. Then in 1964 the Lord led me to the Philippines. In 1972, I was privileged to minister in Japan, Hong Kong, Vietnam, Cambodia, Laos and Korea. In over thirty meetings, I spoke primarily to national businessmen about stewardship.

During the entire month of January in 1975, Juanita and I ministered in South Africa under the auspices of the Free Methodist Church, the Wesleyan Church and the Oriental Missionary Society (OMS). We had twenty-five meetings and eighty decisions for Christ.

Juanita also accompanied me in 1976, from the last of April to the first of June in the Philippines, Hong Kong, Taiwan, Japan and Korea. Our schedule was primarily arranged by Alliance Men. We had over forty meetings with more than 2,000 decisions for Christ.

Then in 1980, my dear lady again accompanying me, we were involved in a concerted outreach in Korea. Astronaut Jim Irwin was on the team as well as Bill Bright of Campus Crusade. Our schedule included Pastor Cho's church, which has the largest congregation in the world. We saw over 3,500 decisions in our time there.

In February and March of 1981, we were in India, Singapore and Korea. Juanita and I also passed through Switzerland and Germany, enjoying some rest and relaxation en route. In just eighteen meetings we saw well over 3,000 salvation decisions.

During July of 1983, Juanita and I visited the Billy Graham Conference on Itinerant Evangelism in Amsterdam. It was good to be ministered to, instead of always occupying the platform. We had fellowship with national

119

evangelists from all over the world. Just before Christmas in 1983, the two of us spoke at a missionary convention of The Christian and Missionary Alliance where we had nine meetings and nearly sixty decisions.

In October 16 through 26, 1984, Juanita and I visited England, Ireland, Scotland and Wales, speaking at churches supported by the Oriental Missionary Society. We had just over thirty meetings with more than forty decisions.

Juanita accompanied me on most of my overseas trips from that time on.

In 1986 it was Puerto Rico again, sponsored by The Christian and Missionary Alliance to speak to businessmen and in national churches. In February 1987, we held a Soul Winner's Seminar in Alaska. Then in May of that same year, our daughter Prudy and her surgeon husband Darrell accompanied us to Korea, for OMS-sponsored businessmen's banquets and church services resulting in over 300 decisions for Christ. We also had the special privilege of meeting with evangelistic teams sponsored directly by our company in Lima.

It was family togetherness time in May of 1989, when our daughter Candy and her husband Paul joined us for outreach in Korea, Thailand, Singapore, Indonesia and Australia. We witnessed nearly 600 decisions during that trip.

Our interest continued to be worldwide, with special heart interest in Asia and Africa over the next several years. My wife and I majored on trips to South America. In January of 1994, we went to Colombia. In August there was a national convention of Christian Businessmen of Brazil, plus banquets and churches with a great harvest of souls.

In 1995, at the invitation of the outstanding Christian businessman T.B.F. Thompson, we made a special trip to Ireland where, again, the Lord honored us with decisions.

It isn't often one has the opportunity to do personal witness overseas, primarily because of the language difficulty. I have stood many times on a street overseas and seen multitudes of people pass by, and have sorely realized the barrier between us through difference of language. Fortunately, in more and more countries now, they are learning English. Even so, it is in one's native tongue where spiritual communication is most effective.

On our 1981 trip, however, I did have an interesting experience on a flight between Madras, India and Singapore. I sat across the aisle from an Indian gentleman counting a large amount of U.S. money. Presuming him to be comfortable in English, I gave him a copy of my testimony.

I leaned back and took a nap. The moment I awakened, I looked toward the aisle and saw the Indian man waiving the brochure to gain my attention. "I want to give my life to Jesus Christ the way you did," he said.

I found a couple of empty seats, motioned for him, and we sat together for I suppose an hour. He had been to the United States studying to be a chemical engineer and wanted to tell me all about it. A Dallas businessman had sponsored him, and he was brimming with gratitude.

"I believe in God," he said. "I have heard of Jesus Christ. Now I want to become a Christian." It was quite easy to take him step-by-step through the gospel to the moment when he opened his heart to Christ. I thank God for many such experiences He has given me. But I realize the most effective way to win souls in overseas areas is through the local people themselves. That's why Juanita and I have invested our stewardship in the training of Christian workers overseas.

In January 1996, we went back to South America, to Bolivia, and in September of that same year to Peru and Mexico. Then in 1998, I went alone to India for the twenty-fifth anniversary of the Every Creature Crusade Teams in India. I spent July 16 through 27 in Brazil to minister in a revival spearheaded by a Brazilian pastor I had met in India.

As I said, one of the purposes of our trips was reconnaissance. As a farmer keeps an eye on his crops or a businessman checks his points-of-sales, so we needed to see where the money being generated by our business was being used. Not that we wanted to tell missionaries what to do, though we occasionally did make suggestions, but the main reason was to give us specific people and programs to include in our prayers. As our ministry grew, it was a great joy to, as much as we could, follow each detail of missionary outreach with prayer.

It was in January 1955 on our trip to Medellin, Colombia, when a crisis came into my life. The opportunity was given for me to give the three concluding addresses at a series of revival meetings in one of the churches. But from the moment I began speaking, I experienced a spiritual equation different from anything I had ever encountered. Not knowing Spanish, I delivered my message through an interpreter and it came to me forcefully that the missionary who related my words to the audience in their own tongue did so with unusual unction.

At the close of my talk I said, "God is present here tonight. He speaks with deep conviction to many of your hearts. Let us bow our heads. If the

Lord has spoken to your heart tonight, step out of your pew and come to the altar here at the front."

Immediately, people began to come. There had been nothing emotional about my presentation except for urging those present to receive Christ and make Him central in their lives. Many of the people who came forward were in tears. My wife attests that neither of us had ever seen anything quite like it before nor since. It was magnificently spontaneous.

Usually when a speaker concludes his speech, he sits down, since he has finished giving his message. I couldn't sit down. I stood as though riveted to the floor, for I had once again reached a milestone and was having a significant encounter with God.

"What is the most important thing in the world to you?" I heard the Lord say to me. Looking down at the altar, I silently replied, "The most important thing in the world to me is to see people seek Your face, Lord, in response to the Holy Spirit's blessing upon my testimony."

"Stanley, if a soul is the greatest value in all the world, then what investment can you make that will pay you the greatest dividends 100 years from now?"

For a moment, it seemed as though I could project myself 100 years into the future, and from that vantage look back upon a panorama of my life. I saw the home I owned, the money in the bank, the investments I had in a couple of other companies. I saw the plans I had for future earnings. I was giving God sixty percent of the profits from our business and doing exceedingly well with the forty percent coming to me.

"What are you asking me to do, Lord?" I prayed silently. It was a precarious question to ask.

"Stanley," I could hear God's unmistakable voice in my thoughts, "if you agree that a soul is the greatest value in the whole world and is the only investment you can make in this life that will pay dividends for all eternity, would you be willing to go back to Ohio and become an employee of Mine?"

"An employee, Lord? Isn't that what I am now?"

"We're *partners* now, I want you to turn your business completely over to me." I was stunned.

"On the cross," I heard my Master saying, "I paid the supreme price that you might become My disciple. Are you willing to give all that you have in order that others may come to know Me and serve Me the same way you do?"

I bowed my head over the pulpit. Observers doubtless thought I was praying for those at the altar. I was so captured by the struggle of my heart, however, I was oblivious to those people, to the church, to the fact of being in South America. I don't know how to explain the awe of that moment.

I'm such an ordinary person. I make no claim to a special connection to heaven other than having access which is available to any Christian. I mean to glorify my Lord as I say that when a man does seek to involve God at the center of his life, he can expect divine encounters.

A pragmatic streak runs through my normal thought pattern. I told you I'm not a sentimentalist, but I have to insist I was dealing intimately with God those moments on that platform. If you doubt it, then I would like an explanation of why my own mind would generate a suggestion so completely at odds with my own selfish interests. It had to be God. He was asking me to turn my entire business over to Him. It's incredible beyond anything I had ever considered in the realm of stewardship and commitment.

Could I do it?

The desk in my office wouldn't be mine anymore, not even the pen used to sign my name. For nineteen years I had lived, eaten and slept the business. I had gone through its birth pains, saw it now growing into glowing success. A businessman thinks of his business every waking hour and plans a year or more in advance. It's his life and his security. Now God asked me to turn it all over to Him.

"OK, Lord," I managed to pray loudly from the silence of my heart, "If that's what you want, I will obey. As a businessman I agree this is the wisest investment I can make."

I didn't tell anyone.

"It was a wonderful meeting," my wife said when we were alone in our room. I nodded.

"I was praying for you," she continued.

"Were you?"

"Of course I was." She looked at me inquiringly. I smiled, knowing she had not understood my question. But I did not offer an explanation at that moment, but instead I walked to the window and looked down on the street. A trio of Indian women sat complacently on the sidewalk in the light of a bright street lamp, their backs against an adobe wall, chatting amicably about matters of the day.

"Something bothering you?" Juanita asked. I kept silent. She didn't press her curiosity further and we retired.

I awakened early the next morning. Frankly I didn't feel very well. You know, you can experience spiritual shock as much as physical. After breakfast I took my Bible and slipped outdoors to a secluded tree.

"Lord," I prayed aloud, "I can't do it. I can't go back to Ohio and turn my business over to You. Isn't sixty percent enough? Many Christians don't so much as give You ten percent." Even as I prayed, conviction returned to my heart.

"Perhaps it was an emotional decision I made last night, Lord," I said. The conviction grew stronger. "Then You must show me definitely, give me positive direction from the Bible. Please, God, let me be absolutely sure."

I've already told you what I think about simply opening your Bible and finding directions from the Lord. Yet that morning, among those beautiful trees, I did just that. My Bible opened to Matthew 13:45-46: "The kingdom of heaven is like a merchant seeking beautiful pearls, who, when he had found one pearl of great price, went and sold all that he had and bought it" (NKJV).

That settled it. The Holy Spirit had once again used the Bible to convey my Heavenly Father's message to me. And so on January 15, 1955, I told God I would no longer be a stockholder in either States Smelting and Refining Corporation or the United States Plastics Corporation. All stock would belong to Him. I would merely be an employee.

My wife had been wonderful in the past when partial stock was relegated to our foundation, but my courage waned when I realized I must tell her of this final step. Yet I should have had no apprehension, knowing what the reaction of this superb partner the Lord had given to me and our ministry would be.

"You know how much I believe in you, Stanley," she said, controlling her emotions. "How could I live with you all these years, see you every morning on your knees for an hour talking to God and getting instructions from Him, and then question what He tells you now as we are in the very heart of one of the mission fields so near and dear to us?"

"A prudent wife is from the LORD," states Proverbs 19:14 (NKJV).

Back home when we asked our lawyer to finalize the arrangement, he said, "I will agree only on the condition you make your wife at least a part-time employee to protect the two corporations in the event of your sudden death." We did as the lawyer advised.

"Honey, if God is going to own the business," I said, "we need to give Him room to expand." She agreed.

In 1955, we had purchased property outside of Lima, so we decided to build a new plant, four times larger than the old one. We planned the structure so that in itself it would give a tactful and distinctive witness for our Lord.

It stretched for 200 feet along US 30, one of the highways so integral to my earlier years as a traveling salesman. At one end we had three tall windows representing the Trinity—God the Father, Jesus Christ the Son and the Holy Spirit. Next to the windows in stainless steel lettering on a solid stone background, passersby could read, "Christ Is the Answer." Three posts on the canopy at the main entrance stood for the life, death and resurrection of Jesus Christ.

We could not at that time have realized that in 1976 we would start all over again, this time building a new factory with five acres under roof. It's a magnificent complex, but it's not ours. It belongs to God. If Juanita and I were ever again to own our business, we would be compelled to buy back the stock certificates from our Heavenly Father.

During all these years, I maintained my prayer partnership with Art Arthur. I cannot emphasize the joy that is ours as we look back over the years and thank God for the decision we made to turn all of the assets over to Him.

Suppose Juanita and I had kept the stock? We had more than several million dollars in profits each year, after taxes, and as the business grew, much, much more. For what? A home in Florida, investments, a beautiful mausoleum in which to be interred one day? A man can only eat one meal at a time, wear one suit at a time, drive one car at a time. I have all that now. Isn't it enough?

It is, and I have no desire for more. Instead, my wife and I have sent it on ahead. We live comfortably and extremely happily. We have all we need and are transmuting the efforts of this life into eternal stocks and bonds.

To God be the Glory!

CHAPTER

TWENTY

The OMS International Story

I need to backtrack to show you the amazing way in which God led us to the heartbeat of our stewardship involvement in missions overseas.

In 1952, our church invited the well-known Dr. Dwight Ferguson to hold a two-week revival meeting. God had used Dr. Ferguson in the Houghton College revival and on several other college campuses as well as in many churches.

Revival broke out in our church—there was standing room only. One night there were seven pastors from other churches in our city who came to see the revival. Two weeks went by. Normally the meetings would have terminated, but the revival continued. Many nights the altar would fill up even without any preaching. Revival came to my own heart.

One day the evangelist said to me, "The Oriental Missionary Society (OMS) has invited me to go to the Orient, Taiwan, Japan and South Korea to minister in the great awakening that is going on there. Why don't you go with me?"

To make the story short, I went, was to be gone six weeks, but it was three months before I got back home, my heart overflowing with the aftermath of an unprecedented spiritual experience.

One afternoon prior to leaving on the trip to the Orient from Los Angeles, I was invited to the residence of Mr. and Mrs. Charles Cowman, cofounders of the Oriental Missionary Society. Mrs. Cowman is the author of the widely used daily devotional book, *Streams in the Desert*. I spent the afternoon with her and then she prayed for me before I left her. I received a special anointing from my meeting with that prestigious and saintly woman.

Our team consisted of Dr. Dwight Ferguson, Mr. and Mrs. Byron Crouse and myself. We flew to Hawaii where we had ten days of meetings under Youth for Christ. Then we had meetings in the Philippines, Hong Kong and on to Taiwan. We took a train from Taipei south to Taichung where our first target meeting began.

OMS seemed to specialize in homey, colorful compounds. The missionaries, mostly Americans, struck me as among the friendliest people I had ever met. I looked forward to the fellowship and ministry outreach with greatest anticipation. But then tragedy changed everything when Dr. Ferguson received word that his son had been killed on a hunting trip. Though stricken with grief, the sorrowing father took care to solidify continuing arrangements. "I have real peace in my heart that you can carry on yourself here, Stanley," he told me. I did not refute him, although my self-confidence had plummeted. When Dr. Furgeson's plane took off for New York the following morning, I felt awesomely helpless and no small amount frightened. But, as He always does when we trust Him, God intervened.

The meetings were very difficult. They were attended by nationals and by refugees from Mainland China. Byron Crouse, the song leader, and I spoke through two interpreters. I would make a statement, which the first interpreter translated into Hakien, the language of Taiwan. The second interpreter then translated my statement into Mandarin, the predominant language of the refugees. It was enormously awkward.

"I don't know how this is going to go," I said to Byron just before the service. "Take as much time as you possibly can. And pray for me!"

After my first meeting, I said to one of the interpreters, "Do you think the people got anything out of my message?"

He looked at me very seriously and said, "Do you think you can do better tomorrow night?" The next night, I asked him the same question. Slightly smiling this time, he repeated, "Do you think you can do better tomorrow night?" It was a great relief when those meetings were over.

Next, we traveled to Kaoshung, the most southern tip of Taiwan for another series of meetings. I was so happy when they were over. From there, we moved to the middle of the island to Hsingchu, to a church that was divided because two missionary organizations were claiming the same church. Friday night we had our first meeting—dead as a doorknob, no movement and no interest. I was to speak again Saturday night and Sunday morning and evening. I was feeling desperate.

Saturday afternoon, the rest of the team went to tour a broom factory, but I didn't want to go. I locked myself in my hotel room. I had to meet God for these meetings. Hour after hour went by with no victory.

At last God spoke: "Nothing plus God equals God."

"That's it, God! You take over the meeting tonight." That night the altar filled, with the same thing happening on Sunday morning and again Sunday night.

From Taiwan I went to Japan. Gloriously, there was more of the same, with people responding to the gospel invitation night after night. Then I saw something that changed my entire life and my goal—the Every Creature Crusades. Utilizing national Christians armed with army maps, OMS was visiting every home on every island and the mainland for the second time with the Gospel of John. They went door-to-door, explaining the gospel and inviting people to a gospel tent meeting at night. We saw multitudes of Japanese being converted.

The Every Creature Crusade concept soon occupied my heart. A few years after my trip to the Orient, we received news that OMS had depleted its budget for Every Creature Crusade, and they were forced to cancel the program.

"What a shame," I told Juanita. "Every Creature Crusade must certainly have been on the Lord's agenda when He gave the great commission to His followers." Time passed. I waited hopefully for news that OMS had given the movement a restart. They didn't.

"We've got to do something about it," I told my wife. After much prayer, I got an idea and went promptly to call on Dr. Ermy, president of the mission. "If I can trust God for $50,000 a year," I said, "will you start the Every Creature Crusades up again?" He assured me they would.

That was over a decade ago. Contributions to the mission from our business went from $50,000 a year to $100,000, then $300,000, then $1 million, $2 million, until this year it's over $3 million. The Every Creature Crusade has spread to nearly thirty countries, with over 600 teams involved. In one year alone they recorded over 80,000 decisions, with over 100 new churches being started.

The Every Creature Crusade touched the ministry the Lord called me to pursue back in 1945, to be a personal soul winner, and a ministry he called me to in South Korea in 1952. "Ask of me, and I will give thee the heathen for your inheritance, and the uttermost parts of the earth for thy possession" (Psalm 2:8, KJV).

Life's Greatest Goal—Winning Souls

I would like to share with you some of the opportunities the Lord provided me for personal outreach. As you read these experiences, keep in mind that what the Lord permitted me to do He can also enable you to do. Remember too you are not the soul winner—the Holy Spirit is. You are simply the tool the Holy Spirit can use—and will use—as you reach out to others in personal evangelism.

You may remember this first story from our motion picture, *The Answer*. The president of an oil-refining company in Texas called me one afternoon asking if he could see me the next day. Promptly at 9 o'clock the following morning, he entered my office.

"Mr. Tam," he began, "how do you know when your sins are forgiven? How do you know when Jesus Christ comes into your life? How do you really know that, when you die, you are going to heaven?"

I explained the gospel to him, but my attempt at giving answers seemed only to incite more questions from him. He paced the floor, thinking, asking. Then, after two hours, he suddenly said, "I understand now. I want to pray. Is it all right with you if we get down on our knees?"

We did just that, I kneeling beside him, listening as he confessed his sins and prayed, "Jesus, I now receive you as my personal Savior."

As he left and returned to the airport, he said, "Thank you for your help. I've found the peace I have been searching for for so long. But I don't understand why I had to come from Texas to Ohio to find it." I didn't know for sure, either, but I was very glad that God had guided this man to me and that I could play an integral role in his turning to the Lord.

Back when I was using a motion picture projector to show Christian films as a means of witness, I stopped at one house where the lady at the door said, "We have a Bible class meeting at our home just now. Jehovah's Witnesses. You're welcome to join us."

I excused myself and left. I made numerous return visits to the couple and found them receptive each time. I showed them several Christian films with strong messages, each time hoping they would come to a saving knowledge of Christ. Slowly, but without any argumentation from me, they saw the error of the Jehovah's Witness cult and one night both received Christ as their Savior. We followed up on them and got them into a church. Their two daughters were converted, and I also had the privilege of leading their son to Christ. Their son went to a Christian college and became a Baptist minister.

It isn't practical to carry around a motion picture projector anymore. But both of our films, *God Owns My Business* and *The Answer*, are on video and available for your use. All you need to do is check the video information request, together with your name and address, on the response card included at the back of this book.

As my prayer partner and I met every noon to talk to the Lord together, we discussed opportunities for witness. We decided to begin a Bible class for unsaved people. We held the class at my plant. In six months, however, we had only seven people attending, all of them born-again believers. Many unbelievers were invited but seemed afraid of the idea.

Then a businessman who owned a furniture company responded to our invitation. He told us he was a Christian and that he was looking for this kind of fellowship. Fellowship he found, but also a clear presentation of the Bible such as he had never heard before. As a result, he became a born-again believer.

Attendance swelled in the class to as many as seventy people on a Thursday night. Over 100 received Christ as their Savior. One timid lady, who lived about twenty-five miles away, heard about the class and came. "Do you permit Catholics?" she asked. We welcomed her warmly.

Our strategy was to serve light refreshments after the class, at which time those of us in charge would sit by those who appeared to be unbelievers and visit with them. It took a while for the Catholic lady to understand the gospel, but one night she accepted Christ. She began to win her family and as of this accounting, nearly twenty of her family members have opened their hearts to Christ.

A distraught woman called to tell me her husband had attempted suicide and was in the hospital and asked if I would please go see him. I did, finding the man with badly slashed wrists and so full of tension and unfulfillment he had decided to end it all. But there in his hospital room, it was my privilege to guide him in the sinner's prayer.

His wife became Juanita's prayer partner. Years later, when this lady passed away, her family insisted I officiate at her funeral.

On the short flight into Chicago one day, a mother and her four-year-old daughter sat beside me. I began to receive a burden for the woman's soul and realized I had only those few minutes in which I could speak to her, so I immediately began to talk to her.

I found her to be of the Catholic faith, quite sure she had established her relationship with God through her church. But she listened when I presented the gospel and became quite troubled when, as we neared Chicago, I asked if she would consider receiving Christ as her Savior.

She answered with a blunt, "No." It seemed she did not mean to be rude but was simply convinced her church had met her need, but I could sense a hint of uncertainty in her eyes. I could feel us beginning to descend into Chicago and assumed my opportunity for further witness was gone.

But then an announcement came on the airline's public address system that the Chicago airport had just shut down because of the weather, and we wouldn't be able to land. The pilot was searching for an alternate site.

This gave me a good half hour to continue speaking with the lady. She began to cry. When I again asked if she would consider receiving Christ as her Savior, she replied, "Yes, I would." It was a beautiful experience and the brief delay didn't hinder me from getting to my evening appointment on time.

I've had many witnessing adventures on airplanes. One involved an NFL football star on a flight to Korea. My daughter Prudy and her husband were with me. Shortly out of San Francisco, I introduced myself to the prominent athlete and began giving him my testimony. One of the flight attendants heard us talking and politely interrupted our conversation to say, "I'm a born-again Christian." Then she introduced us to another flight attendant who was also a believer. This made an obvious impact on the football player.

Long before we reached Seoul, Korea, I had the pleasure of helping the football player pray his way to Christ.

* * *

There is never a dull moment in soul winning. For example, there was a sign painter who frequently did work for us who had resisted salvation for several years. He often made it a point to chat with me, invariably introducing the subject of religion. He seemed to delight in making me feel he was just ready to yield, only to turn bluntly away.

One night when he came to do some work, his face was black and blue. He had been drunk and had gotten in a fight and apparently received the worst of it. He was subdued all evening. After he finished his work, I offered to buy him a milkshake. He agreed and we drove to a fast-food location. When we finished and sat in the car, I said, "Wouldn't this be a good night for you to pray, right here in my car, to accept Christ?"

"No," he said.

"Why?" I asked.

"If I ever get saved," he answered, "I've decided it must be at the altar of a church."

I thought about inviting him to our church the following Sunday night, where he could be sure of an altar call. Then one of those rare, off-beat ideas struck me.

"I've got the keys to our church," I told him. "Let's go. You can kneel at the same altar I did when I was saved." He responded to the idea with an approving smile, so we drove to our church, parked and entered. I turned on the lights above the altar, leaving the remainder of the church in subdued darkness. I wish someone could have been there with a camera and with a recorder, too. He was so very ready and truly genuine.

* * *

I spoke to a Christian woman's group banquet in Houston. As I sat beside the chairwoman at the head table, she told me her husband gave her much concern and said he was not born again.

"Those of us in charge of this banquet are in a fellowship together later this evening," she continued. "If you could meet my husband, would you consider talking to him?" I assured her I would. She deftly arranged it so that, after dismissal, I was to ride with her husband to the residence selected for the fellowship, which was about a twenty-minute drive away.

"When did you become a Christian?" I asked as we began our journey.

"Oh," he said nonchalantly, "I'm not a Christian. You see, I have a problem. If I became a Christian, I couldn't go to church with my wife because her church doesn't believe in evolution." When I avoided the evolution subject and got straight to the gospel, I discovered the man had a genuine spiritual hunger. There in the car, he prayed the sinner's prayer. I explained the importance of openly confessing his faith to others, and asked if he would be willing to tell his wife's group of friends what had happened.

"I sure will!" he replied.

When we reached the designated residence, about twenty people had gathered in the large living room. Before I could so much as introduce the new convert, he blurted out, "I have just received Jesus Christ as my Savior!" The women were stunned for a moment, but then they were overjoyed. They hugged him, kissed him and welcomed him joyfully into God's family.

* * *

I received a letter from an Arab gentleman in California, president of an electronics firm.

> We like your products but haven't appreciated the pamphlets you put in your shipments, also the inside cover of your catalog. We have had a lot of discussions about these things. But I feel different about it now. I have been converted as a result of reading your literature.

* * *

In my book *God Owns My Business*, I mention the George May Company of Chicago, one of the finest consulting firms in America. They were a great help in organizing our business. One of the top officials saw the inclusion of the company name in the book and bought 250 copies, instructing each of the company's representatives to show the book excerpt to prospective customers as part of his or her sales pitch.

Subsequently, I got a letter from one of the ladies of the firm in which she said,

> I've carried your book for over a year, but the only page I've ever read is the one that talks about our company. Two nights ago I decided to read the book for myself.
>
> Something happened and my whole world began to change. I've been a chain smoker, and I seemed to lose my taste for tobacco. I took pills to wake me up in the morning and put me to sleep at night, and became addicted. Yet, after I finished the

book, I found myself sleeping like a baby at night and waking up as chipper as a young colt every morning.

I decided to go see a clergyman. I found a church, went in and talked to the pastor about what had happened to me.

"Lady," he told me, "you've been converted to Christ!"

* * *

I sometimes think the Lord deliberately allows refreshing and stimulating things to happen to those of us who witness as an encouragement and for our enjoyment. For example, a Dr. Stalbaum in Lima heard I was going on a trip to South America and asked if I would be willing to go see his nephew. He didn't know what country he was in, but it was somewhere in South America.

I put it out of my mind. Then, weeks later, I spoke at a breakfast meeting in Medellin, Colombia. After the benediction, a young man came up to me and asked if we could speak further about Christianity. So we arranged a time, with the result that the man became a believer. As he was about the leave, he said, "I understand you're from Lima, Ohio. I wonder if you ever heard of my uncle there? His name is Dr. Stalbaum."

* * *

I attended a direct mail catalog seminar in Chicago and passed out my catalog for critique. I received a barrage of criticisms for the "preaching" it contained. I was given fifteen minutes to give my testimony, and then I offered free copies of my book *God Owns My Business* to anyone who might be interested.

Weeks later I received a telephone call. "I was one of those who criticized your catalog in Chicago," the caller said, "and you gave me one of your books. I took it home, tossed it into a dresser drawer and forgot all about it. Several months later, I was watching television, and your film based on the book came on. It really caught my attention. I went to the dresser drawer and got out the copy you gave me and began to read. I couldn't put it down, I was so fascinated. When I finished it, in the middle of the night, I gave my heart to Christ."

* * *

Juanita had surgery and was placed in a room with another woman, an unusually pleasant individual, to whom I witnessed. The woman said she wasn't ready. Then, as Juanita was being checked out of the hospital, I became so burdened, I got an addressed postcard, went back to the room and gave it to the patient.

"When you are ready to receive Christ," I said, "send this card to me." After some months, the card arrived. Juanita and I went to the lady's house and led her to Christ.

The longer I served the Lord in soul winning, the more sensitive I became to His timing. Though He is the God of the ages, our Heavenly Father has a unique sense of clocks and calendars, as illustrated by a subsequent event involving the woman with whom my wife had shared a room at the hospital.

I received a phone call from her one day stating she had a friend in the hospital who appeared open to the gospel and she wondered if I would be willing to see her and help her.

I was busy and almost replied that I would need to put it off. But as I often do, I sensed an urging in my heart, so as soon as I could find an opening in my schedule that day, I drove to the hospital.

It was almost a casual encounter, so open and ready was the woman to receive salvation. In my humanness, I felt a bit irritated. "There's surely no rush," I told Juanita when I returned home. "It could have easily waited a day, until things settled down at the office." Or could she? That next evening, when I returned from work, Juanita had the evening newspaper ready to show me. Opening to the obituary page, I saw that the woman I had led to Christ the previous afternoon had died within hours after her spiritual victory.

WHAT IF . . . ?

A clergyman in Burbank, California received a copy of *God Owns My Business*, through a book club. He wrote and asked that if I were ever to visit California to please schedule his church for a meeting. It so happened I would be in San Diego in a few days but could not possibly arrange a night for Burbank. So I urged the pastor to come down to the San Diego meeting, which he did.

"I've been a pastor for thirteen years," he told me, "but I've never received Christ as my Savior." That day he did it and became so excited he returned to his church and led eighty-four of his members to the Lord, plus his wife and two sons! The one son became a missionary in Columbia, South America. The minister was so amazed at his own transformation that he went down to the *Los Angeles Times* newspaper and told them his story. They ran a front page feature.

I tell you, friend, winning people to Christ is the most exciting thing I know!

* * *

As I told you, we have a sign on our building plainly reading, "CHRIST IS THE ANSWER." A number of people driving on Interstate 75 alongside our property have seen the sign and turned to the Lord. A number of them have come to tell us. We can only imagine how many have done so without telling us.

One salesman came in to see me and said he saw the sign for the first time and began to weep so profusely he had to pull over to the side of the road, where he prayed and received Christ into his heart.

* * *

A truck driver had engine trouble, pulled up and stopped just outside our place, vaulted the fence and came to our office to call for mechanical assistance. I met him in the hall, where he told me he would have a two-hour wait for a mechanic to arrive. When I asked him if he had seen our sign on the building, he told me his wife was a Christian and was praying for him and that a friend had just been to his home and tried to get him to become a Christian.

He told me he lived in Knoxville, 400 miles to the south, and that he had actually had the feeling of running away from God. But the Lord knew what to do about that, causing his truck to break down just outside our property! That day the man prayed to receive Christ as his Savior.

* * *

Another man who came to see us told me he had driven past our factory several years and always laughed when he saw the sign. But then he began to have financial, health and marital problems. Wondering if Christ really was the answer, he prayed, "Jesus, save me." Several years later he came to see me, to tell me how the Lord had met the needs in his life, healing his body, mending his marriage, improving his business and, most importantly, saving his soul!

* * *

Another salesman by the name of Bill Hanes came driving down Interstate 75 , saw the sign and turned off the exit. As though led by invisible escort, he drove to our plant and, meeting me, told me he was a member of the

Kiwanis and they had commissioned him to find a layman who could give a talk at their Easter week session. Seeing the sign, he presumed I would be able to fill such an assignment.

Fortunately I had the date open. He was about to leave and I asked him if he had any spiritual need. He told me he was a chain smoker and, with the warnings about cancer, had tried desperately to quit but couldn't. Then, too, as a salesman, he entertained a lot of clients and, as a result, had become an alcoholic. He had even gone forward in a church but, in spite of his sincerity, continued the chain smoking and heavy drinking.

"Well, it sounds to me," I told him, "that you went forward seeking reformation instead of salvation." We looked into the Bible together. I showed him verses such as Romans 1:16, "I am not ashamed of the gospel of Christ, for it is the power of God to salvation for everyone who believes" (NKJV) and Second Corinthians 5:17, "If any man be in Christ, he is a new creature: old things are passed away; behold, all things are become new" (KJV).

As we talked, he told me he couldn't believe in hell. Obviously this was a distinct barrier to his search for spiritual peace. When I showed him the account of the rich man and Abraham in hell, he became very embarrassed.

"I didn't know that was in the Bible," he said sheepishly. He then understood his need and, with an open heart, cried out to the Lord for forgiveness and salvation. The following Sunday night, he entered our church and gave public testimony. Bill Hanes illustrates something I find to be strategic in soul winning: In order to get men saved, you must first get them to realize they are lost.

* * *

There was a photographer in Lima who regularly used our silver collectors. After sending in a silver-covered unit, we would mail him a replacement, always including Christian literature. These he promptly tossed, unread, into a nearby wastebasket.

His eighteen-year-old daughter became ill. Medical tests revealed her illness to be terminal, giving her only a short time to live. He returned, stunned, to his office, where he found a fresh silver collector on his desk. In the package, of course, were several gospel tracts, which he did not throw away this time but, instead, gave them several readings. Then he called me, asking if he could come to our house and talk to me. As a result, I had the privilege of leading him to Christ.

* * *

After God healed me from cancer, which you can read about in the next chapter, my doctor insisted I have an annual physical. In fact, he would put me in the hospital for two days to allow time for all the tests. During one of those checkup times, I occupied a bed alongside a man who was so uncommunicative I decided not to disturb him. But then the Holy Spirit began to bother me so incessantly I knew I had to talk to the gentlemen. So I introduced the conversation. Although he didn't converse with me, he listened. When I introduced the gospel, his interest heightened. When I invited him to open his heart to Christ, the communication barrier went down completely.

"Lord Jesus," I heard him cry with distinct sincerity, "I know I am a sinner. I believe Jesus died on the cross for my sins. I accept Him now as my Savior."

It was plain to see he had really done business with God! That night I fell soundly asleep, but was awakened at about two in the morning by a loud scream. One of the night nurses, making routine rounds, discovered that the man in the bed beside mine, whom I had been privileged to lead to the Savior, was now in that Savior's presence!

* * *

For many years, I was active in the Sunday school of our church, making a point of visiting parents who sent their children but did not themselves regularly attend. By way of contrast, I began to notice a young man who came week after week. So I talked to him, and asked if I could come visit him in his home. He agreed. When I arrived at his home one night that following week, his wife told me he had not yet returned. I explained my reason for coming, that I was so pleased to see Bill regularly attending Sunday school.

She began to laugh, and said, "Don't think too much of it. There's a reason for his attending and it isn't because he likes Sunday school. In fact, he doesn't. He hates when he has to bring the children.

"The reason he brought the children," his wife continued, "was he wanted to buy some fishing tackle and I said he could only do it if he took the kids to Sunday school for three months, relieving me of the responsibility."

My optimism sagged. Soon he returned from work, and before I could get in a word edgeways, he began to criticize the church, the phoniness of church members and such things. Then he brought up something about politics, remarking how corruption thrived in our city. This gave me the opportunity I had been looking for, and I began talking about how men's hearts become corrupt. He softened, but I was young as a witness at that time and had difficulty keeping his attention.

I asked if I could return the following week and bring one of my films, to which he agreed. After I showed the film, however, he went into a tirade criticizing it for its poor quality and confusing message. Even so, I tried to speak to him about salvation. But he got up abruptly from his chair and said he didn't want to hear any more. But he did tell me I could return in a few days.

I prayed much during that time and determined to do my best the next time I saw him. When I returned, he met me at the door with a wry grin on his lips. "You're just wasting your time," he said.

My heart sank.

Then he burst into a broad smile as he said, "I was saved last Saturday night. I was taking a bath and got to thinking about all the things you told me. The Lord really convicted me and right there, sitting in the tub, I accepted the Lord as my Savior!" Years later he became our Sunday school superintendent.

* * *

I took my projector and films to one home where a man was somewhat rude. It was the early days of television and, even though I set up my projector and began showing a film, he refused to turn off his television.

But, determined to be persistent, I returned several times, always facing the same television problem. Then one night I came and discovered the television was in for repair. I began setting up to show him a film on the plan of salvation, but he stopped me. For a moment it appeared he would once more reject my witness. To the contrary, however, he told me that—even though he had been rude and left on the television when I showed films other times—he had seen enough of the message to have a clear picture of his need for Christ. A few moments later, we were on our knees together as he opened his heart to the Savior.

* * *

John Fisher sold and rented office equipment, specializing in typewriters. We gave him a considerable amount of business. During his various visits, I witnessed to him, but he was resistant. Then the time came when Art Arthur, my prayer partner, and I began a Thursday night Bible study at our plant. Quite apart from us, another man invited John to the Bible study. John's brother also came with him, and the two began to attend regularly.

We prayed for several months, and the two men came to understand the gospel and one Thursday night received Christ as their Savior. They grew rapidly as Christians.

One day John came to our plant to show us a new adding machine. All of a sudden, he turned pale, told me he didn't feel well and thought he'd better go home. On the way home he had a heart attack, crashed into a telephone pole and was dead before they got him to the hospital.

"Prepare to meet thy God," the Bible admonishes in Amos 4:12 (KJV). Unless you have experienced it personally, you cannot possibly understand what it means to lead someone to Christ and then see that person prepared to meet his God when the time comes for him to die. I am thankful that I was able to lead John to give his life to the Lord before his death.

* * *

From my years of experience, having often given a testimony in evangelical churches, my conviction has been reinforced that being a member of a good church does not insure one's relationship to the Lord. In one church, when I gave the invitation, a man came directly to the altar. I recognized him as the church treasurer.

He told me how he had moved into the community to come to this church, led a good moral life, was honest and faithful to his family. Everyone presumed he was a Christian. So he played the part. For many years, he carried the load of realizing he wasn't really right with God. But that night at the altar of the church where he was a member, he genuinely joined God's family.

I spoke another night at a large liberal church in nearby Findlay, Ohio. It was the dead of winter, with persistent sleet making driving, and even walking, precarious. Response at the meeting was like the weather outside. No one came to talk to me, though I had earnestly prayed for at least one soul out of that needy group. I waited for anyone who might want to come and talk to me. No one did.

The entire group departed. So I also left and headed for the parking lot. The janitor closed and locked the door behind me. I wanted to get to my car, to avoid the sleet and head homeward. But just as I entered the parking lot, a lady stepped into my pathway.

"I'm not happy with the things you said tonight," she said by way of introduction.

"I'm sorry," I began, "but—"

Interrupting me, she continued, "You asked if we died tonight, did we know we would go to heaven? Well, my problem is I know I wouldn't go to heaven."

What do you do with a woman in a dark parking lot on a windy, sleeting night? That problem was resolved when she said, "My husband is over there in our car. He feels the same way I do."

Relieved to hear that her husband was nearby, I suggested they permit me to visit their home. She protested that surely I wouldn't want to be out any longer than necessary in this bad weather. When I insisted, she finally gave in and told me to follow them.

In their home, they showed me a stack of sermons obtained from radio preachers. These they had read many times, but had not been able to find the peace and satisfaction they longed for. I shared the gospel with them. They listened like little children. At midnight, we arose from our knees after Mr. and Mrs. Bill Murphy had received the Lord Jesus as their personal Savior.

It was a long drive home that night as I inched my way along the icy highway, but the sunshine of God's presence flooded my heart.

* * *

My wife and I were returning from a speaking tour in South America, and we passed through San Juan, Puerto Rico. While clearing customs, I became acquainted with an army man. We chatted a bit. He was a purchasing agent, and what he had to say interested me.

As soon as we completed the customs formalities, we boarded a tourist flight for Miami. It was one of those planes where the airline packs in as many seats as possible, and this day the passenger cabin was filled to capacity.

I sat at the window, Juanita beside me and another passenger out by the aisle. "Looks like I'm staying right here where I am," I said to Juanita.

"We can't do much moving around," she agreed.

Shortly after takeoff, I noted that five rows ahead of me—also by the window—sat the army purchasing agent.

"Stanley," the Holy Spirit instructed me, "I want you to witness to that man."

"That's impossible," I countered. "How will I ever get to him?"

The Holy Spirit kept urging me until finally I gave in and said, "All right, Lord, I'll witness to him if You'll arrange it."

No sooner had I prayed that prayer than Mr. McKenzie got up and squirmed his way to the aisle, where he walked to the front of the airplane. The pilot had begun calling out the various islands of the Caribbean over which we were passing, and the army man stood looking at a map of the region as he listened.

Taking my Bible with me, I managed my way across to the aisle and up to the front. "Where are we now?" I asked. He pointed to the place on the map. I watched another moment, as the pilot continued his information. Then there came a lull in the pilot's report.

Breathing a prayer for guidance, I whispered to the man, "Sir, I've been praying for you ever since we got on this airplane. Would you like to talk about God?"

He turned to look fully into my face, and I shall never forget the obvious tinge of sincerity in his eyes. "I would," he said. We found a place where we could talk and, in a matter of moments, I had the privilege of leading him to Christ.

* * *

Let me tell you about the time I went without my dinner to win a soul to Christ—a particularly meaningful experience for me, because it involved my elderly Aunt Mabel.

I arrived in Cincinnati for a speaking engagement a bit after 6 p.m. My meeting was at 7:30. I was hungry. But the Lord reminded me how many times I had wanted to witness to Aunt Mabel but she was always with people and I couldn't. So, with that in mind, I went directly to her home and found that she was alone.

As tenderly as I knew how, I said, "I know you've been a churchgoer all your life and a good moral person. But have you ever been born again, Aunt Mabel? Have you ever received Jesus Christ as your Savior?"

"No, Stanley," she said very soberly, "I haven't."

"Would you like to?"

"Yes," she replied. And she did.

I made it right on time for my engagement and let me tell you, food had never been more tasty than when I ate later that evening.

* * *

A young man sitting beside me on a bus told me he had been involved in a race car crash which nearly took his life. The brain surgeon, who spent several hours attempting to repair his skull, told next-of-kin he could not possibly survive. But he did.

"It's been seven months since the surgery," he said, "and during that time I have been trying to find peace with God. But nobody seems able to help me."

"I can help you!" I exclaimed. Joy surged into my heart, realizing this was yet another example of how the Holy Spirit leads a soul winner to someone He has prepared for salvation. And that day, on that bus, Delmar Hewitt received the Lord Jesus as his personal Savior.

* * *

My wife and I boarded a rapidly filling plane in Tampa on our way to Atlanta, where we would make connections north. When the cabin door closed, the aisle seat beside me remained unoccupied. Then, just before we were towed back from the terminal, the door reopened and an elderly lady entered. She was weeping. She came and sat in the aisle seat beside me.

As the plane took off for Atlanta, her sobbing intensified, and I asked her if I might pray for her. This pleased her and she became more calm.

"My daughter is in the hospital in a coma," she told me. "She almost succeeded in committing suicide." The grieving mother resumed crying and I told her there was someone who could lift her burden. I asked if she would like to meet that person.

"I surely would," she replied.

I opened my Bible, initially sharing Luke 24:36 with her, where Jesus said, "Peace be unto you" (KJV), then we went through the gospel and I had the joy of seeing her open her heart to Christ.

* * *

For sixty years, we have put gospel tracts in each shipment that goes out of our plant. We get occasional criticisms but in those sixty years, during which we mailed out 150,000 packages a year, we had had nearly 500 customers write, call or come to see us each year, saying they had received Christ as a result of those tracts.

At a photography convention one time, a man from Ann Arbor, Michigan, stopped by our booth. I had been at his place, heard how incessantly he swore, but had never had an opportunity to talk to him about his spiritual needs.

As he stood at our display area, however, he said he wanted to talk to me sometime. On a hunch, I asked if he wanted to talk about the Lord. To my surprise, he said he did. I arranged for him to come to our room that night. "I never imagined this man would have any sense of spiritual need," I told Juanita, "Whenever I've been in his plant, the air was blue with his cursing."

He came, however, with an open and hungry heart. He said he had read the many pamphlets we had enclosed in our shipments. "I was wondering," he began, "if you could tell me what happens after death. This question has been bothering me for a long time. I figured, from those leaflets you put in our shipments, you could maybe help me."

"I can tell you about life," I responded. "Eternal life." In the end, God gave me the privilege of leading another seeking soul to faith in His Son.

* * *

The Holy Spirit uses different tools to prepare people for conversion. One finds so many useful tracts these days. Let me tell you about an experience I had with a couple who had seen a Christian film and were deeply moved by it. Unfortunately no one had followed up on the message given in that film and the couple had not yet come to the life-giving decision of salvation. I had met the couple at a liberal church in Lima where I was asked to speak to a group fellowship. Walking out to the parking lot, I came across the couple and struck up a conversation.

To the man I asked, "Sir, have you ever had the experience I talked about tonight, of being born again spiritually?"

"No," he replied.

"If you died tonight," I continued, "where would you go?"

Without missing a beat, he said, "I'm a sinner, Mr. Tam, and I would go to hell."

He was agreeable to my suggestion that I go to their home. As we sat in their living room, they began talking about the film they had seen, how they had wept as they discussed its message, but didn't know where to turn for an answer. That night, I was privileged to kneel with them and their teenage son as the three of them opened their hearts to Christ.

* * *

Our business is direct mail, and we have 25,000 items that we sell. Warehousing requires five acres under roof. This, in turn, necessitates a huge amount of racks on which to hold our products. There was one salesman from whom we purchased the racks.

Speaking with him, he told me he owned a saloon in addition to his sales business. Because we did so much purchasing from him, I had many opportunities to talk to him about Christ. Many salesmen will listen to you because they think it's good for business. This salesman, however, listened with what seemed to be real sincerity. I invited him to our weekly Bible study.

It was there, one night after class, that he opened his heart and accepted Christ as his Savior. Without being told to do so, one of his first post-conversion actions was to get rid of his saloon. One day a state patrolman found him parked alongside the road, dead of a heart attack.

People talk about mixing business with religion. That's OK, I guess. From my side, however, I like the idea of mixing business with soul winning.

* * *

Yes, there is joy in soul winning, but there can also be disappointments, even heartaches. For example, as I drove up to our headquarters one morning, I noticed a window in the office area was covered by cardboard.

"We've been robbed!" I gasped. And so we had. The safe was gone and there were papers strewn all over the floor. "Lord," I prayed as I got alone in my office, "help me to know why this happened. Was it so I could lead someone to You? Do You have a special lesson to teach me?"

As it turned out, a young man newly out of reform school had come to me on the pretense of being a believer. He asked me to pray for him because he needed a job. He knelt beside the safe when he prayed. He and his gang had hired a taxi at midnight, come to the plant, broke the window and gained admission.

A couple of months later the safe was found in a stone quarry. Insurance covered most of our loss, but I never had an opportunity to meet that young man a second time.

However, four days later, a salesman came to see me. He had read about the burglary in the newspaper and came to sell me burglary insurance. As I witnessed to him, he told me how his father had mortgaged his business as well as collecting money from others to help a new minister build a church. A new church was never built. Instead, the minister took the money and fled.

The situation turned the salesman away from the church and any interest in the gospel, except that he kept meeting other Christian businessmen in his sales contacts, and began to have a hunger in his own heart for spiritual peace.

He found it that day, and I had the privilege of leading Roger Frazelle to Christ.

* * *

A young couple began coming to our Sunday school and church. They had left another church because they didn't feel the preacher was faithful to the Bible. They certainly seemed to be Christians. And yet, as I talked to them, I sensed a spiritual need.

So I called on them one night and showed a film. They expressed much interest. The wife sat nearest me, so I asked her, "How long has it been since you were born again?"

Pain contorted her face as she replied, "Oh, Mr. Tam, I have never been born again."

"Would you like to be?" I asked.

"More than anything else in the world," she answered. She added that she often came under deep conviction, but could never quite bring herself to go forward to the altar when the invitation was given.

I had the privilege that night of bringing Johnny Miller and his wife to a sure knowledge of salvation. Both became active as witnessing Christians.

* * *

A young photographer came to my display booth one day at the National Photographer's Convention. He had a distinct Southern accent. I felt a keen desire to witness to him.

So, chiding, I asked, "Are you a good old-fashioned Southern Baptist?" He told me he was Methodist.

My next question was, "Are you a born-again Methodist?"

"I don't know what you mean," he said. I began witnessing to him, but we were soon interrupted by a prospect who came wanting to know about silver collectors. Realizing I wouldn't have an uninterrupted time to speak with the young photographer, I gave him a copy of Dr. Walter Wilson's book *Romance of a Doctor's Visit* and asked him to be sure to come back and tell me what he thought of it.

The next day he returned but again there were interruptions, so I invited him to come back at closing time and go to my room where we could have a talk.

He arrived a half hour early. Because he was not the ordinary type of seeker, we chatted nonchalantly for a while. When he mentioned he lived in Chicago on the north side, I asked if he had ever heard of Moody Memorial Church. He hadn't, so I began explaining how he could find it.

"Say," he politely protested, "it's my sins that are bothering me. Let's talk about them." Soon we were on our knees. After he prayed to receive Christ as his Savior, he jumped to his feet. "I feel clean all the way through!" he exclaimed.

* * *

I have emphasized that you and I are not the soul winners. The Holy Spirit is. I see this authenticated again and again.

For example, I entered the plant after closing time one day when a truck driver drove up with a supply of plastic items we had ordered. The driver unloaded them, and seeing me off to one side, came and said there was no one to sign his delivery slip. I signed it for him.

In so doing, I also gave him a copy of my testimony. I waited as he looked it over, and listened as he told me his parents were Christians, but that when he got old enough, he left home so he wouldn't need to go to church.

When I pressed him about making a decision, he said, "I wouldn't do it without first talking to my wife." I explained how God wanted him to be the spiritual leader in their home so it was up to him to take the first step.

He bluntly excused himself and left. I proceeded with some work I was doing on a silver collector when I again heard a truck drive up. It was the same man.

"I couldn't get away from the things you said," he told me, deeply moved. "I got ten miles down the road and decided I better come back." It was a simple matter to follow the Holy Spirit's guidance, asking him to open his heart to Christ, which he did!

* * *

One night I was sick in bed with the flu when I received a phone call from Joe Leatherman, a man I had led to Christ several years before. "I need you to come and lead my brother-in-law to the Lord," he said. "He gave me permission to call you."

I was about to excuse myself when Joe added, "He has terminal cancer."

Joe picked me up and we drove to the man's house. Just as we knelt to pray, someone pushed me aside and joined our circle. It was Joe's sister.

"Pray for me too," she said, weeping. "I want to be saved, same as my husband."

* * *

A cardboard salesman called on us off and on for seven years. He always wanted to see me, and would talk for half an hour or more about religion. "I keep the Ten Commandments," he boasted, "attend church every Sunday, read my Bible and believe in Christ."

I sensed, however, that he was unsaved.

Then one day he came to my office. He became unusually sober as he said, "Mr. Tam, you've got something I want—assurance of eternal life."

"You're like a man visiting a car showroom," I said. "You see a car you like. It's the right color, the right model, the right make. But just standing there admiring that car will never get it for you. You've got to make a transaction and buy it." He was listening intently.

"You are the same spiritually," I continued. "You go to church, read your Bible, admire Christ, but that's not enough."

He got the message, went with me back to our conference room where I carefully explained the way of salvation to him. "I want to make the transaction," he said.

* * *

I cannot overemphasize, as the Bible plainly teaches, that you and I can never be soul winners by ourselves. We can only be tools the Holy Spirit uses if we are obedient to His guidance.

It's like an embarrassing experience I had in Covington, Louisiana, when I spoke at a Christian businessmen's banquet and the next morning in the church. After church one of the members invited me to come and join some twenty other guests for a standup lunch at her house.

I filled my plate and turned to look for a place where I could conveniently stand to eat. I saw an adjoining room which did not have many guests in it. When I proceeded to take a step toward that room, however, I found my way blocked by a man kneeling at my feet. At first I thought something might be wrong.

When I asked him, he didn't speak. A woman nearby said, "He can't believe he's actually seeing you. He doesn't know how to thank you for what happened in his life. You see, he read a copy of your book and as a direct result became a Christian."

I helped the man to his feet, as I said, "You mustn't give the credit to me, sir. I didn't convert you. My book was only the tool through which the Lord guided you." We had a wonderful chat together. I learned he had purchased additional copies of my book and given it away as a witness to others.

* * *

In preparing this chapter, I have asked God to spare any reader from thinking this is some kind of ego trip for Stanley Tam. It's an ego trip for the Holy Spirit and for our Lord Jesus! How fantastic that they let us be the tools through whom they work!

You see, soul winning takes on various forms. It may be through outright conversation. It may be in the giving of a tract, or perhaps through a book. It's important for you and me to be faithful and to obey the Holy Spirit's prompting. "The fruit of the righteous is a tree of life; and he that winneth souls is wise" (Proverbs 11:30, KJV). We have seen three souls per day on an average accept Christ as their Savior for twenty-three years now.

Cancer Crisis

"Bless the LORD, O my soul;
　and forget not all His benefits:
Who forgives all your iniquities,
　Who heals all your diseases." (Psalm 103:2-3, NKJV)

I have always enjoyed good health. In 1976, however, I began to suspect something was going wrong in my body. I was weary from the time I got up until I retired at night. I could hardly pick up my briefcase without pain stabbing into my chest, penetrating my abdomen, sometimes thrusting like a lightning bolt along my spine.

"You've got to see our doctor," Juanita told me repeatedly, having the manifest capability of being persuasive without nagging. "You're a sick man, Stanley," she said.

"Some days I feel fairly good."

"Like today, for instance?" she primed.

"Well . . ." my speaking further gave way to a finger-like sting that probed my chest. So I called him, but he was out of town. I forgot to call back.

Gone most weekends, I returned exhausted each subsequent Monday morning. A date came up which had been on my schedule for several months, a three-state women's convention in Lincoln, Nebraska. There would be 700 present. It was a three-day assignment, with several lectures each day.

"Can't you call and cancel it?" Juanita asked.

"It's getting pretty late for that," I countered. "I should have canceled several weeks ago."

Over my wife's protest, even against my own better judgment, I flew to Lincoln. After the first lecture, I barely stumbled back to my room and flopped onto the bed, setting my alarm clock so I wouldn't miss my next appointment. I fell sound asleep.

Struggling back to the second session, I wondered how I would possibly make it. I learned that Nebraskans are made of solid stuff and are clear thinking with intense motivation. After each lecture, they formed a cordon around me, affirming what I had said, requesting further light on comments I had made. When I could at last break away and get to my room, I felt nauseated and dizzy.

I called Juanita that night, trying not to be overly dramatic about my condition, but she could always read me like a book.

"Can't you cancel and come home?" she pleaded.

"There's nobody to take my place," I contested.

"Are you sure?" she prodded. "Have you asked?"

"Sure, I'd love to be home," I said, "but the Lord is touching hearts here. We've had several ladies come to Him today. I'll see how I feel in the morning."

I fell asleep calling out to God for His mercy and sustenance and, to my joy, awakened the next morning somewhat refreshed. I called Juanita and told her I felt I could make it through the schedule. She reluctantly concurred but assured me she would have a doctor's appointment for me as soon as I got back.

I had a miserable trip home and arrived at midnight. Juanita informed me the doctor wouldn't be able to see me until later in the week, so I remained in bed, sleeping nearly around the clock. As soon as he could, the doctor gave me a thorough physical—including X rays and a consultation with an oncologist. I talked to the Lord almost constantly, clinging to the promises which had been so viable during the years. Even so, I remained apprehensive.

Time dragged. Then, finally, the doctor's office called, requesting that I come in for a summation. "Give it to me straight, doc," I said. "I can take it."

"We have a long fight ahead of us," he told me.

Meanwhile, a lab technician showed Juanita the X rays. Countless spots blemished the film.

"It's all over your body," our doctor told me.

"Cancer?" I asked.

The doctor took a quick breath, turned away sighing. I was struck speechless. I cried out to God for help. He gave me a measure of peace, sufficient for me to ask, "What's my prognosis?" Again, he remained silent.

"Do I have months? Maybe a year?"

"I want you to go directly to the hospital," he replied quietly. "We want to get you in shape for some biopsies tomorrow morning."

"Biopsies?"

"We need to know how pervasive the malignancy is and how best to prescribe treatment."

I called Arthur, my prayer partner. He reminded me of the promise we claimed every time we met for our weekly intercessions. The promise of the Lord Jesus Himself, recorded in Matthew 18:19, where He said, "If two of you agree on earth concerning anything that they ask, it will be done for them by My Father in heaven" (NKJV).

There was a radiance on Art's face when he entered my room later that afternoon. "God has given me real victory," he said. "I believe He's going to heal you!"

The two of us had seen many wonderful answers to prayer in our years of prayer partnership. Often, when we faced some demanding need, God would give Art victory the same way he expressed now. I didn't argue with my good friend. But I did a lot of thinking.

I had been afflicted with what was apparently cancer in one of its messiest forms. Was it possible? Could God really heal me?

"I'm getting people all over town to pray for you," Art said as he left.

Our son-in-law, Wes, informed our fellow workers of my condition and a pall of apprehension spread across the plant. The office staff notified Christian friends all over the world by letters, telegrams and phone calls. Our Christian radio station—of which I will tell you more in the next chapter—spread the news, urging people to pray.

Becky came to be of assistance to her mother, who slipped away for a while with her Bible. Calling to her daughter, she came bounding back, pointing to a reference. "Look what I've found!" she held up the book for her daughter to see.

"The mission board chairman gave me this promise— Isaiah 41:12. Read it, sweetheart!"

"You shall seek them and not find them," Becky read.

"It's those spots, Becky. That's what they won't find. The Lord told me—so plainly I could almost hear His voice!"

Juanita showed me the promise when she returned to the hospital that evening. "They will be sending out the biopsies tomorrow morning," she continued, "and—" She stopped abruptly, then added, "We get the reports back Saturday." A shadow came across my dear lady's face. "Saturday is my birthday," she whispered. Then she began to cry.

"Visiting time is over," a voice spoke from the public address system. We kissed and Juanita left. I was alone.

Sleep evaded me. I turned on my light, took out my Bible and tried to read. It was as though the pages had gone blank. I had a four-hour struggle with the Lord that night, my own Gethsemane experience.

"Search me, O God, and know my heart," I prayed, remembering Psalm 139. "Try me, and know my anxieties; and see if there is any wicked way in me . . ." (NKJV).

"Search," I prayed desperately. "Every bit of me. I confess my sins, my pride."

It was a time of spiritual cleansing, deep and vital and real. I struggled to know the Lord in a new way as my Healer. "I know You as my Savior," I whispered, "my Sanctifier. But can I really take You as my Healer?"

I thought of Psalm 2:8, which the Lord had given me so distinctly in Korea: "Ask of me, and I will give thee the heathen for thine inheritance, and the uttermost parts of the earth for thy possession" (KJV).

I thought of Jeremiah 33:3: "Call to Me, and I will answer you, and show you great and mighty things" (NKJV). The Lord had given that to me as a mandate. Surely it was not yet time for me to die. There was more work for me to do.

Then it happened.

A great peace came over me, so very beautiful and enhancing. It felt as though an internal oil began flowing from the top of my head down through my body all the way to the bottom of my feet. The pain went away, along with the apprehension and uncertainty. It was like the caress of a divine hand!

"Lord," I cried out, my voice surging with joy, "what is this? Have You healed me?" Tears of gratitude came to my eyes. I fell back against my pillow in joyful submission and I slept.

A nurse awakened me early the next morning. I had a moment's apprehension before remembering what had happened during the night. Then peace returned in abundance to my soul.

I was placed on a gurney and wheeled into what appeared to be a small operating room. Immediately the tests began. I soon surmised it was a matter of extended surgery. When I at last returned to my hospital bed, Juanita was waiting for me. Her face was drawn, though she tried to smile. Her voice had a frightened tremor to it, as she attempted to speak, telling me of the many people praying, the messages received. Then, unable to restrain herself longer, she began sobbing.

"But hold it, sweetheart!" I interrupted, reaching out to squeeze her hand. "I've got something wonderful to tell you." We looked at each other a long moment.

"Last night," I began, "I believe God healed me!"

"Healed you?" she gasped.

"Don't you remember the promise God gave you in Isaiah 41:12?" I lightly chided. I explained fully what had happened. I saw hope rise in my wife's eyes. I saw her abandoning doubt and apprehension.

"I've got no more pain," I said. I moved my arms vigorously to demonstrate. "My energy is back. I feel like I could go out and mow the lawn!"

The hours dragged until Saturday. Juanita came to the hospital early, scarcely mentioning her birthday. We clasped hands, spoke little.

Finally our doctor came into the room. I shall never forget the look on his face, the lingering pessimism and yet the obvious wonderment.

"It is absolutely incredible, Mr. Tam," he began. "When I examined you before—the X rays, the tests we did, the oncologist's findings—there was no question in my mind. We took eighteen biopsies, and every one of them showed up negative. There isn't a trace of malignancy anywhere in your body!"

Never before had God shown Himself to be so sovereign in our lives! As Juanita put it, "This is the best birthday I've ever had!"

I immediately resumed my schedule, sensing the unction of the Holy Spirit upon my efforts with renewed vitality.

Decades have passed since my healing. I have annual physicals, and the reports are clean year after year.

I am now midway into my eighties. It has been a quarter of a century since God healed me of cancer. Before I close the cancer chapter, however, I need to share one more thing.

On our numerous trips to Taiwan, we had met a missionary lady by the name of Ms. Fusty. With our busy schedule at the time, we didn't have a chance for any extended fellowship with her, but she had made sure to see us long enough to assure us that she not only prayed for us but continued to pray the more so having met us and seen us in ministry.

Well, within a fortnight of the Lord's special touch upon my body, we received a message form from Ms. Fusty. She was writing to find out if we were all right because some two weeks earlier she had sensed our having great need for prayer. She related this experience:

> One night I went to bed. In the middle of the night, God woke me up and laid you so heavily upon my heart that I was forced to get out of bed, get down on my knees and groan in prayer for you. As time went on, the burden lifted and I got up and went back to bed. I have never had an experience like this in all of my life. What happened to you on the night of October 19? Have you had a crisis, a car accident, have you been sick? Please write and tell me.

October 19 was exactly the night before they took the eighteen biopsies.

Does God answer prayer? Absolutely!

In John 15:7, Jesus says, "If you abide in Me, and My words abide in you, you will ask what you desire, and it shall be done for you" (NKJV). God's answer may not always be what you want, but you can rest assured that whatever the answer may be, it is always the right answer.

First Thessalonians 5:18 states the case clearly: "In everything give thanks; for this is the will of God in Christ Jesus for you" (NKJV).

I know it for a fact!

Sunsets and Horizons

N
ow well into my eighties, you would expect me to be looking toward the sunset of my life.

In a realistic sense, of course, I am. But, very frankly, I'm looking more toward horizons than to sunsets. With the reasonably good health the Lord is giving me and the vast store of experience He has entrusted to me through the years, I look to the future with anticipation from a background of reminiscence.

First, let me reminisce.

One of my early memories is of a family horizon, the death of my Grandfather McBeth. I remember ascending a small step-stool so I could look down into his casket, an awesome, indelible experience as vivid in my mind now as it was when it occurred. As I've already told you, Grandfather McBeth was a wealthy land owner who sold his possessions wisely, thus accumulating a fortune. Quite a contrast he was to Grandfather Tam, who partnered with my father in their ill-fated farming venture.

I was a young Christian when Grandfather Tam died. I had yet to win my first soul to Christ and thus, to my knowledge, both of my grandfathers entered eternity without Christ.

Our Christian and Missionary Alliance pastor preached the funeral sermon for Grandfather Tam, at the conclusion of which my father came to Juanita and me and said he had accepted Christ during the service.

* * *

My mother had four brothers. One of them, Harry McBeth, was the father of Bud, my childhood buddy. Her brother Dwight married Eve and lived in Canton, Ohio. He sold and installed air-conditioners in commercial establishments. He took a liking to me and invited me while I was in high school to live with them, and said he would teach me air-conditioning. Uncle Quay McBeth lived in Florida, so we rarely saw him. Uncle Jim, who lived in Cincinnati, played in a dance band. We made a yearly visit to their home.

I had only one uncle on my father's side, Uncle Glen. He married late in life. He built racing cars out of Model Ts, and he succeeded in souping them up to 100-mile per hour speeds, a phenomenon at that time.

After I gave my life to Christ and became a soul winner, I had a great burden to win him to the Lord. I had to be careful in witnessing to him, making sure I avoided the presence of his wife, who blatantly rejected the gospel.

The two of them did attend a liberal church, and one time when I openly witnessed to Uncle Glen, my aunt came at me like an attacking wild animal. "We'll have no more of that!" she snarled. "Your uncle and I are good church members. If we need to know anything about religion, we'll ask our pastor." As far as I can know, they both died unsaved.

It was Uncle Glen who built the house trailer in which Juanita and I began our married life.

* * *

I consider myself very honored to be named Alumnus of the Year at my alma mater, Shawnee High School. The bestowing of such an honor began the previous year, when famed media star Hugh Downs received the award. I knew him during high school years. His mother and my mother had what you might call a close friendship.

SHAWNEE HIGH SCHOOL

I must not finish my story without telling you a bit about that school's influence on my life. It was an exciting day when I entered as a seventh grader, for the school had just been built. It had the outside look of a fine piece of architecture and the inside newness of a well-designed facility for education.

Some of the teachers read the Bible every day in their classes. Others also prayed. In retrospect, I believe this influence—though primarily more moral than spiritual—made a distinct contribution to my subsequent conversion and commitment.

I had learned the Lord's prayer from those many Sundays at the country schoolhouse church near home. One teacher, noticing my abstinence from bad language, my apparent moral character, presumed I was of religious bent and asked me if I knew the Lord's prayer. I proudly admitted that I did, wishing later I had not done so except that one of my virtues was an absolute abstinence from telling lies.

So, after she had read from the Bible, she frequently called on me to give the Lord's prayer. I came to be known as "Preacher" among many of the students. I disliked that but, as I say, I believe such things influenced me greatly in my later life. Then, too, it was no great encumbrance to be nicknamed in this manner during those times.

As I look back on the past, on the sunsets, I can better understand my horizons.

What if my parents, for example, had not only been unbelievers but flagrantly irreligious? What if they had not taken me to the little schoolhouse Sunday school and church? Except for Bud and his short-spanned zeal, there was no one who might have influenced me toward the Christian life. To the contrary, I enjoyed Sunday school and it did have an influence over my future decisions.

Carried further, what if my parents had not lost the farm but, instead, fertile acres had diverted me from my initial sales efforts? I was loyal to my family and might have given up sales and, instead, directed my full energy and endeavor to the potential of the land.

And, following my conversion, what if I had not met that wise dean at Fort Wayne Bible College but, instead, had enrolled to prepare myself for pastoral ministry? What kind of pastor would I have been? Could the talent which the Lord blessed so I was able to build a multi-million dollar industry have been applied to the building of a large congregation? In my earlier years, before I got into so much traveling, I majored on our Sunday school at the Alliance Church and, as its superintendent, saw it grow in abundance.

No, as I reminisce, I am keenly conscious of the sovereign hand of God on my life from childhood until now. I have no inkling of why He singled me out for the privileges that have been mine, but I am grateful.

I must not conclude my story without telling you about WTGN, our Christian radio station.

In 1966, our church called a new pastor, a Peter Courlas from Dayton, Ohio, where he had been a board member for the second oldest radio station in our state. He talked to me many times about the need for Christian radio in Lima.

"You can purchase used equipment very cheaply," he said, "and be on the air for $15,000." We never realized then that it would be several times this amount of money before we would go on the air.

Art Arthur, my prayer partner, and my pastor formed the nucleus for a governing board. We had some space in our new factory, which Juanita and I donated for the radio use. The reason we so readily got our franchise is because we were only allowed to broadcast over FM, a new medium form in those days. Hardly anybody had it. So we told people if they would support us, we would give them a free FM radio. We gave away 5,000 radios in exchange for financial support.

But we had problems.

Our frequency blocked out other favorite radio stations, causing us to have many enemies in the community. Somebody shot the glass out of the front window of our station. We received many threatening phone calls. But, after a couple of years, we finally corrected the problem.

WTGN is a joy to our hearts and a blessing to our community.

Well, I don't classify this radio ministry as any kind of "sunset," but it does lie—with the warmest of memories—in our past.

Now, as a man in his eighties, I look to the future.

In Isaiah 14:24, the Lord tells us: "Surely, as I have thought, so shall it come to pass, and as I have purposed, so shall it stand" (NKJV). Also, Jeremiah 29:11: " 'I know the thoughts that I think toward you,' says the LORD, 'thoughts of peace and not of evil, to give you a future and a hope' " (NKJV).

Then, too, there is First Corinthians 2:9: "Eye has not seen, nor ear heard, nor have entered into the heart of man, the things which God has prepared for those who love Him" (NKJV). Whatever God's plans, promises and purposes may be for me, I rest in them with contentment and security. Turning from the sunsets now passed, I look forward to the horizons of the future!

* * *

It is so good having our son-in-law Wes Lytle at the helm of our business. Born to missionary parents in Colombia, Wes has a heart for stewardship.

He speaks fluent Spanish, no small factor in today's business world. He shares Juanita's and my heart for missions, loves to see people coming to the Lord and also clearly understands the business, its needs and potential. I am available to assist him in any way I can, but am determined to allow him to run the business on his own—led by the Holy Spirit in the same way I have been these many years.

I still have an office in the plant but have vacated the president's office and, indeed, am also in the process of absenting myself completely from my former moorings.

You see, a few years ago Juanita and I purchased a small factory-sized building about a mile south of our headquarters. We call it the Tam-O-Shanter Manufacturing Company.

First, however, let me give you some background.

Woodworking has been a hobby of mine all my life, beginning back when I was a kid building race cars out of wood. When Rachael, our first child was born, I built her a playpen and a baby tender. I built the bookshelves and other items in our home. In the business, we constructed thousands of bins out of wood. In the silver refining business, we manufactured silver collectors out of wood. Our customers preferred our using cypress for silver collectors. They functioned best when hung in the processing vats.

In 1984, my employees gave me a Sears floor model drill press for Christmas. I was really pleased with it, took it home and it became the first woodworking piece of machinery in the basement. That drill press fomented a desire to purchase a wood-cutting saw. With ease, I began making kitchen items, but to do that right I needed other pieces of machinery, a sander, shaper, bandsaw, jigsaw—you name it—until I had a basement full of wood craft apparatus.

I then began to purchase kits to assemble. But, as time went on, I decided I no longer wanted to merely assemble kits. I wanted to build and design my own furniture. So then, starting from scratch and my imagination, I taught myself to create entertainment centers, desks, chairs, tables, dressers, sewing machine cabinets or whatever. The woodworking machinery is now located at Tam-O-Shanter, where we are developing furniture manufacturing.

My main goal, however, in whatever venue I can find, is to develop a soul winning center. Out at the highway, I have a double sided sign that says, "Are you looking for peace in your heart? The answer is in the Bible. Come inside for a free Bible." We have just put up this sign and we are giving away many Bibles to those who stop. This gives us a chance to talk to them about their soul. Already, thirty-two people have accepted Christ as their Savior. We are praying for hundreds to do this in the future.

Tam-O-Shanter is strategically located so people with spiritual needs can conveniently find me and stop for counsel. How far we will go in the development of furniture manufacturing I can't say. What I can tell you, and that for sure, Tam-O-Shanter will, in God's will and with His blessing, become another soul-winning center.

I like to think of having been a student in the University of Experience these past years, with a minor in business and a major in soul winning. Going over our books, Juanita and I find that during our sixty-five years in business, we have been able to contribute out of the business in excess of $100 million for the work of the Lord. When I think of the value of one soul, and recall the thousands the Lord has privileged us with reaching for Him, it seems completely clear that our best procedure would be to put our full emphasis on personal evangelism. I expect to be speaking at a few more meetings, but can certainly foresee the day when speaking will no longer be part of my agenda.

So there you have it.

I anticipate my real future, my sure horizon, to be continued outreach to lost souls. I hope to be leading a soul to the Lord at the moment He takes me home—whether by the rapture or by whatever.

That's the future I anticipate, the future for which the Lord has been preparing me these many years.

That's my horizon!

Laying Up Treasures in Heaven

In the sixth chapter of Matthew, God tells us one thing to do, and one thing not to do.

> Lay not up for yourselves treasures upon earth, where moth and rust doth corrupt, and where thieves break through and steal: But lay up for yourselves treasures in heaven, where neither moth nor rust doth corrupt and where thieves do not break through nor steal: For where your treasure is, there will your heart be also. (6:19-21, KJV)

I want to talk to you about transmutation, the changing of one value into another value. Alchemists for thousands of years have been trying to change lead bars into gold bars, but they have never been able to do it. But as Christians, we can take our time, money and our energy and turn them into eternal treasures.

How can we do that? Can we take a fist full of $10 bills and give them to God and say, "Some day I'm going to be in heaven, and I want You to put these in Your safe so when I get there I'll have some treasure waiting for me"? I think we all realize that $10 bills won't be good in heaven.

So how *can* we lay up treasures in heaven?

One day in church while the offering was being taken, I heard a little girl ask, "Is Jesus poor?" That simple question got me thinking.

Jesus isn't poor; you and I are poor. We came into this world naked. We brought nothing with us and when we die we take nothing with us. Between life and death, we are merely trustees of the material things of life. One day each one of us will stand before God and give an account of how we have handled the material things of life. How do you think you will measure up?

In 1952, I was invited by OMS International to go around the world to speak as a Christian layman. When the song leader and I got to Tokyo, we had a desire to go to Korea. That was when the Korean War was going on. We thought we had the message for the church that was in war. We went to the Far Eastern Command and asked if we could go. Seven days later the United States Army said we could. They gave us papers. We flew 800 miles to Pusan, Korea. Night after night we spoke in refugee churches. They were nothing like what we have in America.

Night after night we spoke in churches that had no lights like we have or beautiful pews to sit on—they didn't even have heat. We spoke almost every night with our overcoats on. But despite the things the church buildings lacked, the people had something in their churches we didn't have here in America. They had an early-morning prayer meeting from five to six during which the churches were packed to the walls. This was going on in some 800 churches at that time and they continue to have such prayer meetings to this day.

Night after night we spoke in those churches. Every night the altars would be filled with people coming to give their hearts to Christ. It had nothing to do with the speaker: Those faithful believers and their prayers are great soul winners.

You didn't need to put an ad in the newspaper in order to get people to show up at a meeting. All you had to do was open the doors and by 6:30 p.m. the church would be packed to the walls. The Koreans all pray at once. The pastor would get up and ring a bell with all his might to get his people to stop praying by 10 o'clock so they could reach home before the curfew. Do you have that trouble in your church?

Night after night I spoke in those churches in South Korea. One night I turned to the missionary and said, "I can't speak in these churches any more."

"Why, Mr. Tam?" he asked.

"I'm learning something," I explained. "It isn't me that has the message. It's these people. Here I come from rich America, trying to tell these people how to live the Christian life, when I see them living in cardboard boxes and canvas tents, and you tell me hardly a family has escaped death. A mother, a father, a child has been taken by the adverse conditions. You tell me they have lost all their earthly possessions because they have been pushed back and forth so many times by these two armies. I live in a comfortable home, I've never lost any of my loved ones. I've never lost any of my earthly possessions. How can I stand in these pulpits and tell these people how to live the Christian life when they've come through the valley of death so victoriously?"

The next morning, as I came out to the breakfast table at the OMS mission station where only men missionaries lived because of the war, I said to those men around that table that morning, "God's been dealing with me. Would you excuse me today from going with you on your itinerary? I've got to meet God anew in my own life."

As those missionaries left that day, I went back to my room and there I began to pray. "O God, send me back to America a different man. Send me back to burn out for You. Lord, why is it I have such a heavy burden of prayer? Is it because You would have me take a step of faith and double my missionary pledge?"

At that time we were trusting God for $5,000 a year for foreign missions. To double the pledge at that time in my life would have been a great step of faith, but I offered that to God. I didn't feel that He was leading me to double my pledge, but I offered it to Him a second time just to be sure that I was hearing Him properly. It seemed He wasn't interested. Instead He began to change the thoughts in my prayer to the book of Ruth. I began to think about how she went into the field of Boaz and she actually asked if she could work in the harvest.

I think the greatest challenge I could leave with you is to urge you to step out in faith and ask God if you could work in His harvest fields in a new and effective way.

That became my prayer that morning. As I agonized in prayer, God spoke to me and gave me an offer. He said, "Stanley, if you do something, I'll do something. If you will just ask of me, 'I will give you the heathen for your inheritance and the uttermost parts of the world for your possession.'"

I drew back and said, "Lord that Scripture is for a missionary or at least a minister. I'm just a lay person." Isn't it true that we hide behind that sentence, "I'm just a lay person?" I prayed all morning and then God gave me that verse a second time and then a third time. I realized that God meant me because I was the only one there. I turned to Psalm 2:8 and underscored it in my Bible there in Pusan, Korea with these comments:

> November 25, 1952 based on the book of Ruth, but I don't know what it means. It's so great to have been spoken to this morning by the Holy Spirit but I still don't know what it means.

I staggered under that promise. How could I believe God for the heathen of the world? Here I was, just a small businessman back in Lima, Ohio. At that time our business was really just beginning. I had some minus factors in my life. I didn't have the privilege of a formal education. I had graduated from high school in 1933, right in the depths of the depression. That year my parents lost their farm. They lost everything they had in this world, and my mother had to take in loads of laundry for 25 cents each so she could finish putting her children through high school. There I was over in Korea and God gave me the offer, "Stanley, ask of Me, and 'I will give you the heathen for your inheritance and the uttermost parts of the world for your possession.'"

On the plane back to Tokyo, I went to the washroom, and when I came back another person had taken my seat. I told him that was all right and I slipped up to the front to take one of the empty seats that were available.

I sat next to a Korean. I figured if I spoke to him he'd just point to his mouth, meaning he didn't speak English. But I said, "Hello."

He answered back, "Hello."

"You speak English?" I asked.

"Yes," he replied, "my dad told me if I learned to speak English I'd never need to worry about making money. I studied for four years in Shanghai. I'm a businessman."

"Oh," I said, "I'm a businessman too. You know, I have a partner in my business that I'd like to tell you about." With that, I began to talk about Jesus Christ.

He looked up and said, "Oh, I am a Christian!"

"Tremendous!" I responded. "Tell me how you became a Christian." He told me the following story.

"I have an uncle in Korea who is a great Christian. I wanted to be a Christian like my uncle but I kept putting it off. So one night I said, 'Tonight I'm going to become a Christian.' This is the way I've done it. I'm a wealthy man. I have a large home. I've invited all my poor relatives to come live with me. I'm supporting them and sending them and their children to school. In this way I've become a Christian."

I could have rebuked him and told him that was no way to become a Christian, but I wanted to win him for Christ. I said, "Mr. Chung, this thrills me to meet a man like you whose heart pants after God. I see it's no accident my seat was taken back there on the plane. God has arranged it so that I could come up and share with you. Would you be embarrassed if I got my Bible out of my briefcase?"

"No," he replied.

I took my Bible and went through the plan of salvation, and when we came to the end, I asked him if he would like to do what God tells us to do in the Bible? He looked at me and said, "This is what is missing in my life. Yes, I'd like to ask God into my life." There behind those seats on that plane, Charles Chung, the best he knew how, told God he was a sinner and invited Christ to come into his heart.

I said goodbye to Charles in Tokyo and figured I'd never see him again. Tokyo was the largest city in the world at that time. But three days later I had run out of Japanese yen, and a friend and I went downtown to a bank, got in line, and the man waiting at the window turned around. It was Charles Chung. He was as surprised to see me as I was to see him.

We invited him out to the OMS Mission compound and that night he gave his first public testimony about how he had accepted Christ as his Savior on the plane. After that, Charles began to write me letters. He asked me how he could intelligently talk to his wife so she too could know Christ. The next letter had money in it, and he asked me to buy all the Christian literature I could with the amount he had sent. He wanted to learn more about Jesus.

God had said to me back in Pusan that if I would do something, He would do something. If I would just reach out and ask Him for the heathen of the world, He would give them to me. My talk with Charles Chung was my first earnest attempt.

As time went on, I moved on from Korea to Hong Kong. I was staying at the International Hotel. One day I was waiting for a missionary to pick me up in his car to take me out to a refugee camp where I was to speak at a Bible school. I was holding my Bible as I waited when a bellhop came up to me and said, "Mister, what's that book you've got in your hand?" I could have told him it was a Bible but I wanted to talk to him about the Lord. So I said, "Oh, you mean this book here? This book comes from God. In it is the secret of how you can live forever in heaven."

We talked awhile, and then the missionary came and I told the bellhop I'd have to go. I left him with a copy of my personal testimony.

I returned to the hotel late that night, and was retiring when the telephone rang in my room. It was the hotel owner. He said, "Mr. Tam, come to my office, please. I want to talk to you." I told him I had just retired for the night.

He said, "Well, first thing in the morning, then, please."

So the next morning I was ushered into the private office of the hotel owner, and after he went through all the courtesies required of a Chinese gentleman, he reached into his pocket and pulled out the testimony I had given the bellhop the day before.

He said, "I see you are a Christian businessman from America. I've read this paper over and over. I see there are some interesting things in here. I'd like to get all of my employees together and have you talk to them and tell them what's in this paper. How about 3 o'clock this afternoon, when we're not busy? We'll rearrange the chairs in the dining room. I'll get all my employees in there, and you talk to them." I agreed.

I returned to the hotel at 3 o'clock that afternoon to find that the hotel manager had done as he had said: Every chair in the dining room was filled. He said, "I don't have this many employees, but we had some empty chairs so I went out on the street and coaxed some people to come in and fill all the chairs. Now, tell them what's in this paper."

That afternoon I had the privilege of telling them what was in that paper, about how I was converted to Christ and what it meant that God was the senior partner of my business. We had a precious time in that hotel dining room that afternoon.

The next morning as I was leaving I went to the desk at 7:30 to check out. I asked for my bill, but when I looked to see what I owed, it said, "Paid in full, compliments of the hotel owner." It really pays to advertise and it definitely pays to witness.

As I left, the bellhop I first talked to carried out my luggage to the English taxi waiting for me. I still had some good Hong Kong money for a generous tip. I reached into my pocket to give it to him but he threw up his hands and said, "Mister, I wouldn't be able to take anything from you. I'm indebted to you for having told me about Jesus."

God had said to me back in Pusan that if I would do something, He would do something; if I would step out in faith and ask Him for the heathen, He would give them to me. Here was my second earnest attempt.

As time went on I arrived in India. On the last day, I went to Calcutta. I was supposed to have lunch with a friend at 2 o'clock in the afternoon, but I got lost. I couldn't find the restaurant. I'd been there seven days previous, but the restaurant wasn't where it was supposed to be. I couldn't read the street signs either. I was going to be late for my engagement. At the same time, an Indian boy wanted to polish my shoes if that was the last thing he did on this earth. Every time I took a step I was stepping on him. I realized I would never find that restaurant unless I had my shoes polished first so I told the boy to polish them as fast as he could. While the boy was polishing my shoes, a young man stepped up to me and asked if I was from America. When I told him I was, he beamed all over and said he had been to Chicago.

I asked him what had brought him to Chicago, and he told me he had been in the Indian Navy. I told him he spoke English well and asked him if he could read it as well. He said he was a graduate of the University in Calcutta. I gave him a gospel tract with the title, *The Man with the Plan*. I asked him if he was going to be in Calcutta that night. He said he was so I invited him to hear me speak at the Youth for Christ rally. He didn't know about that, but took the tract.

I got my shoes polished, found the restaurant and found my friend. When we left the restaurant, the young Indian man was standing there waiting. He came up to me and said, "Mister, I sure like this article you gave me about the Man with the plan, Jesus Christ." I invited him to come to the Youth for Christ meeting so he could hear more about Him. My friend and I were employing a taxi together, I was going to the Youth for Christ headquarters, my friend was going to Lee Memorial Mission, but when we got in the taxi, low and behold the young Indian man got right in with us uninvited. I started hoping that he would go with my friend. I had been on a train all night and I was looking forward to a little more sleep. But when the taxi stopped to let me off at the Youth for Christ headquarters, he got out with me. I was just about to turn to him and tell him he couldn't come with me when he held up the gospel tract and said, "Mister, I sure like this article."

The Lord spoke to me at that moment and I said, "All right, let's talk. What do you know about the Man with the plan?" He told me that when he was a refugee in Pakistan on two different occasions he had heard missionaries talk about Jesus Christ. As we spoke, we leaned up against a board fence in downtown Calcutta. With thousands and thousands of people passing by, I asked him if he would be embarrassed if I got my Bible out of my briefcase. He said he wouldn't be, so I took out my Bible and we went through the plan of salvation together. As we came to the end, I asked him if he would like to accept Jesus Christ as his Savior.

He looked up at me pitifully and said, "Mister, why do you think I've been following you?"

I instructed him in the prayer of salvation and he prayed with all his might. Afterward, I took him to the Youth for Christ headquarters and told Dick Riley, the director, that the young man had just given his heart to Christ. Dick asked him if he would like to be enrolled in their evening Bible school. He said he would.

Then Dick took me aside and said, "Stan, don't get excited about this boy. These Indians will take the best out of one religion and add it to another one and to another and pretty soon they manufacture their own." He said it would take three months to find out whether the young man was truly born again.

I went back to America and Dick Riley wrote me a letter telling me that the young man truly became a Christian, and through his life he won another fine young man to the Lord.

God had said to me back in Pusan that if I would do something, He would do something; if I would just reach out and ask Him for the heathen, He would give them to me. Here was my third earnest attempt.

I went to Bangkok from Calcutta, and on my last day there I had to get up at 5 o'clock in the morning to catch the plane to Burma. I decided to have my devotions on the plane that day. When the plane took off, I was reading Psalms 8, and I was so weary from traveling it seemed like I couldn't concentrate or get anything out of what I was reading. I was just closing up my Bible when a Scripture stood out, and I reopened my Bible and began to read again. This is what I read:

> What is man that You are mindful of him,
>   and the son of man that You visit him?
> For You have made him a little lower than the
>   angels. . . .
> You have put all things under his feet. (Psalm 8:4-6, NKJV)

When I read that Scripture, the Spirit of God spoke to me and said, "All things are under the feet of Jesus Christ. Why don't you ask Him for the money to go with that promise I gave to you in Pusan, Korea?"

The Lord began to minister to me. Among other things, He began to talk to me about George Mueller, that great man of faith who lived 150 years ago in England. God laid upon him the ministry of supporting 2,000 orphans. You might think that it costs a lot to support your own children, but he trusted God to support 2,000 children. He had a policy where he never told a human being his financial need, and he never published it in the paper. He had a private closet where he went by himself and told his rich heavenly Father his financial need. Over Mueller's lifetime, his rich heavenly Father gave him over $7 million to support those 2,000 orphans.

God said to me, "If I can give George Mueller $7 million to support the burden I gave to him, don't you think I can give you the money to support that promise I gave to you up there in Korea?"

"Ask of me, and I shall give thee the heathen for thy inheritance, and the uttermost parts of the earth for thy possession" (Psalm 2:8, KJV). That day God taught me a great lesson. I have a rich heavenly Father. There is a verse in the Bible that says, "My God shall supply all your need according to his riches in glory by Christ Jesus" (Philippians 4:19, KJV). It doesn't say the church board, it doesn't say Mom or Dad, it says "*my God* shall supply all your needs." I decided that since I have a rich heavenly Father, I wouldn't need to borrow any more money in my business. And for the last sixty-five years of our business, we have had a policy not to borrow any money. I've just gone to the bank in heaven. They have a larger vault there than any other place.

When we built our new factory, five acres under roof, we built it by faith. When we started construction, we had $600,000 cash in the bank. When we finished we had spent over $3 million and it was all paid for and we still had the $600,000 cash in the bank that we had started with. It's just amazing how God will bring the money in if you just trust Him to.

Do you believe you have a rich heavenly father? "My God shall supply all your need according to his riches in glory by Christ Jesus." God had worked a miracle. Have you ever thought it through? Everything God does is a miracle. He created you. Therefore you are a miracle, so you can believe Him for a miracle in your life.

A revival had broken out in my heart as I was flying to Burma, but God wasn't through with me yet. After that trip I was invited by OMS International to go to South America to speak in the countries of Colombia, Ecuador, Peru and Brazil in national churches. They felt that if an American layman would come and speak on stewardship perhaps it would help the churches to become self-supporting. Juanita accompanied me; it was her first trip overseas.

While in Colombia, in the city of Medellin which had a population of over 2 million people, I was to speak in a national church downtown. Saturday evening I gave a testimonial message to a church that was only about half full. Despite the fact that the church was only half full, the Spirit of God came upon that congregation. There was something different about the meeting. As I came to the end of my testimonial message, I said to the people, "God has done something here this evening. We're not going to stand, nor are we going to sing. We will just bow our heads in prayer, and if God has spoken to your heart and you have a spiritual need tonight, and you'd like to slip out of your seat and come to this old-fashioned altar in front of the church, come now."

Just like that, spontaneously, in what seemed like merely a second, the altar was filled, then the front pews were filled, and then it stopped, and no one else came. I'd never seen a response like that before. Usually when a speaker finishes he sits down, but that night God began to speak to me. As I stood behind that pulpit and looked at all those people kneeling at the altar, the Lord said to me, "Stanley, what's the greatest value in all the world?"

As I looked at those people gathered at the altar in that church, I knew the answer. God tells us that one soul is the greatest value in all the world. His Word says, "What good is it for a man to gain the whole world, yet forfeit his soul?" (Mark 8:36). Do you believe that? Do you believe that one soul is the greatest value in all the world?

Then God spoke to me a second time and said, "Stanley, if a soul is the greatest value in the world, then what investment can you make in this life that will pay you the greatest dividends 100 years from now?" At that moment it felt as though I traveled 100 years into the future and turned around to look at my life. I saw the home I owned, the money I had in the bank, the investments I had in two companies.

I realized as I had never realized before that the material things we fight so hard for in this life go back to rust and dust if not into the hands of someone else. There would be only one investment I could make that would pay dividends a hundred years in the future, and those would be spiritual things because the spiritual things are eternal.

Then God spoke to me a third time and said, "Stanley, if a soul is the greatest thing in all the world, and the only investment you can make in this life that will pay you dividends 100 years from now are the spiritual things, would you be willing to go back to the States Smelting and Refining Corporation and turn your entire business over to Me and use the profits to spread the gospel around the world?"

I began to argue with the Lord. "Sixty percent of the company already belongs to You," I protested. "Isn't that enough?" The Lord spoke to me once more and I'll never forget it.

He said, "Stanley, on the cross I paid it all for you, that you may have eternal life. Now you're My disciple and I live within you. Can you do less than what I've done for you?" That hit me where it hurt. I bowed my head over the pulpit. I suppose the people in that church in Medellin thought I was praying for those who had come forward, but I wasn't. God was asking me to go back and sit at a desk that wouldn't be mine anymore. You'll never know the struggle that was mine that night unless you go through it yourself. But as I was struggling I guess I thought of this: Wouldn't it be wisest to give to God something I couldn't keep anyway? One day death would come, I'd have to go and leave it all behind, but if I turned everything over to Him, I could transmute it and send it all ahead.

I ask you that same question. Can you do less than what Christ has done for you? One day He gave all for you that you may have eternal life, and now He says you are "bought at a price" (1 Corinthians 6:20). You are not your own anymore. You are to glorify God in your body and your spirit, which are His.

The greatest blessing in a church service is when they pass the offering plate. The money you give to God is the only money you'll ever keep. Your offering to God is like mutual funds: When you give it to Him, it multiplies.

Actually, you don't give God anything. Let me prove it to you. Suppose you had $1,000 and took it to the bank and deposited it in your name. Then you heard that the bank loaned it to someone to help buy an automobile. Do you reason, then, that you don't have any money in the bank because it's been spent on an automobile by someone else? No, if it was deposited in your name, you can go and withdraw it at any time because it's yours and it's in your name. Scripture says, "Lay up for yourselves treasures in heaven" (Matthew 6:20, NKJV). The word "yourselves" means it's deposited in your name.

Of course, if you're not going to heaven, you don't need to do it. But God says if you are going to heaven, then you should lay up yourself treasures in heaven.

"Oh," you say, "Mr. Tam, when Christ went to heaven, He went to build me a mansion. That's all I'm going to need." But have you ever moved into a house that had no furniture in it? God says lay up for yourself.

There is a purpose in laying up treasures in heaven: You'll need it when you get there. And if you don't do it, God considers it disobedience.

The Lord got through to me that night and I said, "Lord, You can have it all!"

Now I don't want anyone to feel sorry for me, because that night I made the neatest business transaction I've ever made in my life. But I do have a confession to make. The next morning when I woke up at the OMS mission station, I thought *This morning I'm just an employee*. I didn't feel so good. The decision hit me a little differently the day after I made it.

I didn't want to talk to anybody, so after breakfast I went out by some trees with my Bible and said, "God, I don't know if I can do this or not. It might have just been an emotional decision last night. Unless You give me something from Your Word for me to stand on, I don't know if I can do this."

I don't think it is a good idea to just let your Bible fall open and start to read, but I didn't want to pick out the promise: my business was at stake. My Bible fell open that morning to Matthew 13. I looked down and saw two verses that had never meant much to me before, but that morning they stood out to me like a beacon. This is what I read:

> The kingdom of heaven is like unto a merchant man, seeking goodly pearls: who, when he had found one pearl of great price, went and sold all that he had, and bought it. (Matthew 13:45-46, KJV).

I take this passage as being a reference to the Church, for God gave His all for the Church. As I read that, I realized that God was telling me that He had given all for the pearl—the Church, the invisible body of Christ—and He was asking me to do the same.

God expects you to do the same thing too. He gave His all for you. Now you are "bought with a price." You are not your own. You are to glorify God in your body and Spirit which is His.

It took me three weeks to tell my wife I had given away her half of the business. Before we got to São Paulo, Brazil, I told her, "Honey, I have to tell you something before I speak in this church tonight. You don't own any of the business anymore, I gave it all away." She took it so well that, on our way back from South America, I said, "Sweetheart, if God's going to own the business, we ought to give Him some room to expand it." So when we got home we built a new factory. We did not know then that we would need to build an even larger factory in 1977.

Because we wanted to glorify God in the architecture of the new factory, we put three tall windows which signified the Trinity, and then across the solid stone part we put CHRIST IS THE ANSWER in stainless steel letters. Across the front of the office we put seven groups of windows to stand for the perfect number in the Word of God. The three posts in the canopy stand for the life, death and resurrection of Jesus Christ. If you come up to our front door you can read our cornerstone which says, "For no other foundation can anyone lay than that which is laid, which is Jesus Christ" (1 Corinthians 3:11, NKJV). Inside there is a missionary map of the world with many lights on it, for that's where God broke my heart.

Back in 1936 I went into business and I went broke. But out of the ashes, defeat and failure God said to me, "Stanley, it doesn't need to be a disappointment. You don't need to go broke. Turn it over to Me and I'll make it succeed." So I can't take the glory for the success of my company because I'm the one who went broke, and He's the one who succeeded.

Now I want to teach you the greatest lesson on stewardship that I have ever been taught. Let me take you back to Pusan, Korea. In 1952 I tried to double my missionary pledge from $5,000 to $10,000 and God said He wasn't interested. You know why? Because I asked Him if He wanted me to do it.

God said, "No, I don't want you to do it. I want to do something through you. I want to give you a ministry and, if you will accept it, I will make it possible."

And that's one of the greatest truths God has ever taught me: *It is not what we do for God, it's what He wants to do through us.*

God said to me, "Stanley, I want to give you the 'heathen for your inheritance and the uttermost parts of the earth for your possession.'" That's in your Bible as a promise to you too.

Well, the day came when we were able to give a one year pledge of $500,000 dollars, then it went to $600,000, then to $700,000 and keeps going up to $1 million.

At the writing of this book, our goal is $4 million per year.

We have an omnipotent God!

Why do we struggle when He says, "Just let go, I'll do it through you"? It is God that works in you both to will and to do His good pleasure. We need to move from the street called Poverty to the street called Faith.

There is a Scripture that says:

> For the eyes of the LORD run to and fro throughout the whole earth, to shew himself strong in the behalf of them whose heart is perfect toward him. (2 Chronicles 16:9, KJV)

You say, "Mr. Tam, that leaves me out. I don't have a perfect heart."

Oh, but you can have a perfect heart. The story goes of a bricklayer who took his son to work with him one day. When he was called to the telephone for a half hour or so, his son had laid a whole row of bricks just as crooked as they could be, but he looked up and said, "Daddy, I wanted to help you."

And he looked at his son and said, "Son, you have a perfect heart toward me."

We all can have a perfect heart toward God.

Does God have something new for you? He does. Are you tired of that squirrel cage life you live in, where you go to work and come home and you eat and go to bed so you can get up the next morning and go to work? When you look at your life, do you have a profit for the kingdom or is your life all centered around yourself even though you are a Christian?

The greatest challenge I could give to you is that you reach out in faith and ask God to let you work in His harvest field. We are all different, like the tools in a toolbox, but each tool has its purpose, and they are all needed to build a house.

He needs you. Let go and let God do a new work in your heart and life. Take a new step for Him so you may be more effective in your service to Him. Ask God to put you to work in His harvest field in a new and effective way. I challenge you to try. Do you think you can win the world by simply sitting on a pew on Sunday? God wants to work through you, to do His will in His good pleasure. Will you give Him a chance?

There is a Scripture in the Old Testament—Deuteronomy 8:18—that says, "It is [God] who gives you power to get wealth" (NKJV). Then He tells you the reason He gives you wealth. So His word may go forth!

How to Receive the Gift of Eternal Life and Become a Vital New Person

One of America's leading evangelists stated that he believed that fifty percent of those who attend church have only received Christ with their intellect and never with their heart. They never received the gift of eternal life and are headed for hell the same as the outright sinner.

> My Friend,
>
> You don't need to be lost. God sent His Son, the Lord Jesus, into the world so you can be saved by receiving the gift of salvation and eternal life. You *can* be sure you are saved and going to heaven.
>
> R. Stanley Tam

In order to receive the gift of eternal life, you must first realize that man is doomed. Jesus said, "Ye are of your father the devil" (John 8:44, KJV). To whom did He say this? To the religious people of His day, the Pharisees. They constantly went to church, they prayed every day, they fasted every week, they paid their tithes, they probably were more religious than you and I, but Jesus said, "Ye are of your father the devil." Being religious is not enough.

What happened that made man the doomed creature he is now? God created Adam and Eve perfect in body, soul and spirit. But when Adam and Eve sinned in the Garden of Eden, the Bible tells us they died spiritually, inheriting a sinful nature. They didn't get it from God, they got it from the devil. They ended up in the wrong family.

The history of sin is found in Romans 5:12. God's word says, "Just as through one man sin entered the world, and death through sin, and thus death spread to all men, because all sinned" (NKJV). Because Adam and

Eve sinned, they became "dead" spiritually. "All have sinned and come short of the glory of God" (Romans 3:23, NKJV).

The Bible teaches that sin is part of man's nature. Therefore, when Adam and Eve had children, their children inherited their same sinful nature. And this is true for every person born since that time. The Bible says, "Our righteousnesses are filthy rags" (Isaiah 64:6, NKJV). You are still unregenerate regardless of how moral or how good you are, and you still won't go to heaven. You will go to hell.

You don't go to hell because you lose your temper, lie, cheat, use drugs, smoke, drink or other bad habits. You go there because you are born a sinner—you are in the wrong family! You are lost spiritually, because of Adam and Eve, our first parents, who sinned and died spiritually.

If you stop losing your temper, lying, cheating, smoking, drinking and other bad habits, would that make you a Christian? NO. You would still be a sinner by birth—you have a sinful nature. You are still in the wrong family, because you have original sin.

Is there any hope? Yes. If you want to go to heaven, you must choose to enter into the family of God.

How do you do this? First, you must confess and forsake your sins. "If we confess our sins, He is faithful and just to forgive us our sins and to cleanse us from all unrighteousness" (1 John 1:9, NKJV).

Jesus said to a preacher by the name of Nicodemus, "Unless one is born again, he cannot see the kingdom of God." Nicodemus said, "How can a man be born when he is old? Can he enter a second time into his mother's womb and be born?" (John 3:3-4, NKJV) Jesus said, "You don't understand. That which is born of flesh is flesh. You have had the physical birth, I am talking about a spiritual birth. Marvel not that I say to you, you must be born again of the spirit. Born from the family of the devil into the family of God, by receiving Christ as your Saviour." (John 3:7, author paraphrase).

The Bible says that there is no eternal life in good works, church membership, water baptism, communion and the other rituals of the church. God has given to us eternal life and this life is in His Son, Jesus Christ. He that has the Son has eternal life; he that has not the Son has not eternal life. Eternal life is in Jesus. If you want eternal life you must accept Him into your life (see 1 John 5:11).

If you accept Him with only your intellect—just your head—you will not experience the spiritual new birth. You must accept Him into your heart, with your whole life. He wants to sit on the throne of your life.

"But as many as received him, to them gave he the power to become the sons of God" (John 1:12, KJV).

The secret of accepting Christ is saying, "Jesus, I surrender my whole life to you, from this day on, I belong to you as my Lord and Savior."

The test of whether you have fully accepted Christ as your Lord and Savior is in this verse. "Therefore, if anyone is in Christ, he is a new creation; old things have passed away; behold, all things have become new" (2 Corinthians 5:17, NKJV). This will be the evidence of the new birth.

How do you know when Christ actually comes into your heart? God's Word says in First Corinthians 3:16, "Know ye not that ye are the temple of God, and that the Spirit of God dwelleth in you?" (KJV). Christ comes into your heart by faith. He is so real that you pray to Him, sing to Him and joy will spring up in your heart with love for Him.

Will you pray right now and invite Christ into your heart, by faith, and become a new creature in Christ Jesus? By praying the prayer and accepting Christ by faith as your personal Savior onto the throne of your life, you are now in the image of God—body, soul and spirit.

The prayer to pray is on the last page of this book. If you will return this post paid card, we will send you FREE, the famous book by Robert Cook *Now That I Believe*. This book tells you how to get a good start in your Christian life.

Now that you have asked Christ into your heart, you have the gift of eternal life because eternal life is in Jesus Christ, and Jesus Christ is in you by invitation. That is why, were you to die, you'd go to heaven.

Thank Him for coming into your life.

DISTRIBUTE 30 COPIES OF THIS BOOK
AND WIN SOMEONE TO CHRIST

Stanley Tam's books have a long publishing history. For every 113 copies circulated, there has been a recorded spiritual decision. We know of no other Christian books with this kind of record.

We also realize, of course, that many results are unrecorded. If there is a recorded response for every 113 books, then we believe that there are at least one or more unrecorded.

This may be the most unusual reason for choosing a case size, but Christian Publications, Inc. has carefully chosen to have this new edition of Stanley Tam's book packed in cases of thirty books.

We sincerely believe that the careful distribution of thirty books is likely to produce an important decision for Christ.

For that reason, we have prepared for you:

THE CARING CHRISTIAN DISCOUNT OF 50%

on one case of
Stanley Tam's Incredible Adventures with God
(For larger discounts on quantity orders,
call 1-800-537-9724 or fax 1-800-854-5498)

Please clip and mail

- -

Please send your check along with your name and address to U.S. Plastics, Inc., 1390 Neubrecht Road, Lima, Ohio 45801.

Name _____

Address _____

City _____ Zip _____

Please send me _____ case(s) of *Stanley Tam's Incredible Adventures with God*.

☐ I enclosed herewith $112.45 for each case ordered. I understand that these books are not to be sold, but given away.

(30 books at $7.00 each, less 50% . . . $105.00. Please add $7.45 for postage and handling on each case, total $112.45.)